WIMPOLE HALL

Cambridgeshire

David Souden

THE NATIONAL TRUST

The main text was written by David Souden; chapter six by
J. F. Fuggles, Libraries Adviser to the National Trust; chapter
seven and the picture entries by Alastair Laing, the Trust's
Pictures Adviser; and chapter eight by David Adshead,
Assistant Historic Buildings Representative for East Anglia.

I have received considerable help from many individuals and
organisations in the production of this book. Oliver Garnett
and Margaret Willes commissioned and shepherded it.
Gervase Jackson-Stops generously lent me the notes and files
on Wimpole from his admirable earlier guidebook of 1979.
David Adshead and John Maddison were unfailingly helpful
in giving advice and time. Graham and Olga Damant,
Administrators of Wimpole Hall, gave me access wherever
and whenever I wanted it, and provided much help and
information. The archivists and librarians who are the
guardians of papers and maps relevant to Wimpole were
always kind and prompt in their assistance. Many friends,
acquaintances and correspondents offered advice, information,
leads or anecdotes. It was under Barry Windeatt's watchful
eye that I joined the National Trust, at Wimpole Hall in its
first year of opening. My wife Nicola helped in so many ways.
This book is for her.

David Souden

First published in Great Britain in 1991 by the National Trust
© 1991 The National Trust
ISBN 0 7078 0139 7

Photographs: Art Institute of Chicago page 15; British Museum,
Department of Prints and Drawings page 11; Cambridge University
Collection, Aerial Photography page 81; Conway Library page 26;
Country Life pages 7, 21, 25; Courtauld Institute of Art pages 14, 82;
John Harris page 17; National Portrait Gallery pages 8, 19; National
Trust/Lanhydrock archives page 40; National Trust Photographic
Library/Andreas von Einsiedel pages 1, 4, 13, 18, 23, 31, 53, 55, 57, 59,
61, 65, 69, 77, back cover; NTPL/A. C. Cooper page 35; NTPL/Roy
Fox pages 24, 32, 42, 43, 44, 45, 47, 48, 68, 72, 74; NTPL/Rupert
Truman front cover, pages 49, 51, 83, 84, 86, 87, 93; NTPL/J. Whitaker
pages 12, 79, 89; NTPL page 76; Sir John Soane's Museum
pages 30, 33.

Designed by James Shurmer

Phototypeset in Monotype Lasercomp Bembo Series 270
by Southern Positives and Negatives (SPAN), Lingfield, Surrey (806)

Colour reproduction by Aculith 76, Barnet, Hertfordshire

Printed in Italy by Amilcare Pizzi s.p.a.
for the National Trust, 36 Queen Anne's Gate, London SW1H 9AS
Registered charity no. 205846

CONTENTS

The tomb of Sir Thomas Chicheley (d.1616), the father of the builder of the first Wimpole Hall, in the Chicheley chapel of Wimpole church. The builder is said to be one of the kneeling figures on the side of the tomb

CHAPTER ONE
EARLY HISTORY

Wimpole (sometimes spelt Wimple) is the greatest country house in Cambridgeshire, and one of the finest in the eastern counties. Its long, brick-built principal front spreads across the top of the parkland as seen from the main Cambridge–Sandy road; and one day, when the replacement trees for the great avenue that was devastated by Dutch elm disease have matured, the southern prospect of Wimpole will again be an incomparable sight.

The road to Cambridge is one of the reasons why the Wimpole estate has long been so important. It is Roman, and within a few hundred yards of the point where it crosses the line of the Wimpole avenue, it joins the great Roman road of Ermine Street from London to Lincoln and York – the old Great North Road. Two miles to the north, the prehistoric route of the Mare Way marks the upper boundary of Wimpole parish and estate.[1] Communications with London have helped to make Wimpole one of the few important landed estates in a county otherwise singularly devoid of them; and London connections have underwritten Wimpole since the later Middle Ages.

Historically, the Wimpole estate has been formed by almost all of the parish of Wimpole, and much land in surrounding parishes (see Chapter Ten). From the twelfth century until the end of the fourteenth, the principal Wimpole manor had been in the hands of the Bassingbourn family. It then changed hands a number of times during a period of fifty years until acquired in 1428 by Henry Chichele, Archbishop of Canterbury and founder of All Souls College, Oxford. Before he died he settled the main estate in 1436 on his great-nephew, also called Henry (although his version of the family surname is spelt Chicheley). Thereafter, the manors that made up Wimpole were gradually transferred into the Chicheleys' hands as part of their long process of land accumulation in the county. One

manor came in 1548 with the marriage of Thomas Chicheley's son Clement to the daughter of Sir John Hinde, Justice of the Common Pleas, and another was bought from the Wingfield family in 1651. Only one other manor, Wratworth on the site of a deserted village, escaped their grasp; it was finally united with the Wimpole estate in 1686, when the Chicheleys themselves were forced to sell up.

So for 250 years the Chicheley family dominated Wimpole and south-western Cambridgeshire. In addition to their landowning interests they had City connections, especially with the Grocers' Company. The first visual record of their house and estate comes relatively late in that timespan, in 1638, when Benjamin Hare drew his detailed map of Wimpole. At the centre stands the main Wimpole manor house, a four-gabled building set within a rectangular moat and approached through a pair of gatehouses. Around it was a small deer-park of some 200 acres, divided in two, on the north and west of the house; the Low Park contained three avenues of trees, the first sign of the sequence of great gardening schemes that were to transform Wimpole. There is now no trace of the original house, since, soon after the map was drawn, it was demolished by Thomas Chicheley, who began to build afresh just to the south-east of the old site.

Thomas's father, Sir Thomas Chicheley, had died in 1616 and shortly after the younger Thomas had come of age in 1635, he began to construct the new Wimpole. Around 1640, the county historian John Layer noted that 'Thomas Chicheley Esq lord of this village is now constructing an extraordinary curious neat house near the ancient site.'[2] The house was extraordinary because it was in a new style; quite how far Chicheley got is difficult to say since the events of the Civil War rapidly caught up with him. Elected MP for Cambridgeshire in the Long Parliament of 1640, in 1642 he took the King's side and moved to Oxford with the Court and the Royalist army. There he had his portrait painted in martial breastplate by William Dobson, and in 1646 he was one of the signatories to the surrender of the city. He was heavily fined, and lived under a cloud until the Restoration – although not in penury, since he was able to marry the widowed Lady Savile in 1654.

Lady Savile had been the heroine of the siege of Sheffield Castle in Yorkshire, when she had held out against the forces of Parliament until her own soldiers persuaded her to give up since she was on the point of giving birth. Her enemies were so impressed that she was guaranteed her freedom –

which she used in furthering the Royalist cause by acting as a spy. Her wealth may have allowed Chicheley to continue the process of land acquisition. After 1660 he blossomed, as MP for the county and subsequently for Cambridge, as Commissioner and then Master-General of Ordnance, as a knight and Privy Councillor.

Wimpole also blossomed. At some point, probably in the late 1650s, the new house was completed; Sir Roger Pratt, the gentleman-architect in the vanguard of the new style of the mid-seventeenth century, gave Wimpole qualified approval in his discussion of house architecture, specifically in

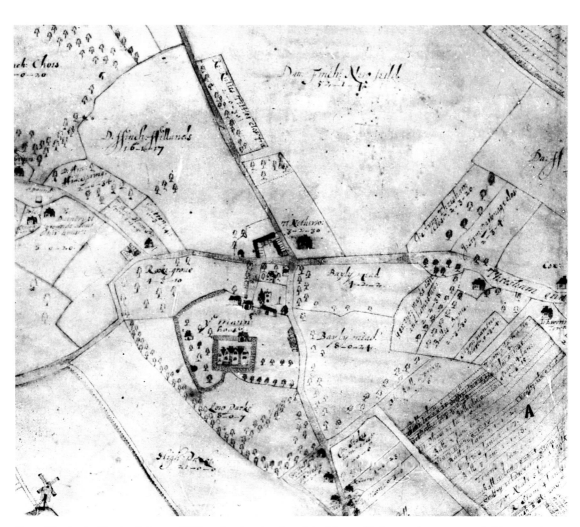

Part of Benjamin Hare's 1638 map of Wimpole, showing the original four-gabled manor house surrounded by a moat

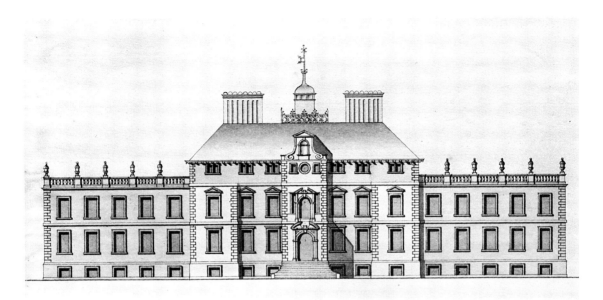

Flitcroft's survey drawing of the south front in 1742. The central block formed the original Chicheley house

relation to that 'most commodious' style, the double-pile house. 'I conceive', Pratt wrote, 'a double building to be the most commodious of any other for so the rooms will neither be so hot in summer, nor cold in winter.' In Chicheley's house, he thought, some of the irregularities apparent in other designs had been smoothed out.

Chicheley produced a house whose innovative plan contributed to the development of the typical later Stuart country house. In the conventional H-plan, two wings flank a great hall entered at one side through a screens passage, as at Elizabethan Montacute in Somerset. At Wimpole the H was turned through ninety degrees. The wings became parallel ranges connected by a block containing two staircases. This allowed not only for a symmetrically placed hall entered through the centre of the south range, but also for a long gallery above, which stretched from the north front to the south. It was but a small step from this arrangement to the true 'double-pile' house like Belton in Lincolnshire, where the parallel ranges were set back to back, with staircases at either end.

The seven-bay house with its massive cellars still stands at the core of Wimpole Hall, heavily overlaid with the building exploits of Chicheley's successors. Its form is best seen from the west side, looking down on the double roofs of the house from the slopes in the parkland. The general appearance of the south front of Chicheley's house can now only be gauged by the measured drawings which Henry Flitcroft made in 1742, prior to refacing and Palladianising the front; the scrolled and pedimented centrepiece recalls a house of the 1630s like Raynham Hall, Norfolk; the elevation, hipped roof, central lantern and chimney stacks another mid-seventeenth-century house, Thorpe Hall, near Peterborough. It is possible that Peter Mills, who designed Thorpe Hall and the buildings of the 1650s at Pembroke College, Cambridge, gave expert assistance to Chicheley (although it must be acknowledged that Mills had deep Parliamentary sympathies). There is, however, more than a suggestion that Chicheley may have been his own architect; certainly, he was regarded as sufficient an amateur in the arts to be among the Commission that toured the dilapidated St Paul's Cathedral just before the Great Fire of London, although his and Sir Roger Pratt's suggestion that the existing fabric be reused was soundly squashed by Wren and other members of the Commission.

Sir Thomas Chicheley lived in great style at his house in Covent Garden when in town. Samuel

Pepys remarked on Chicheley dining 'in the French manner all; and mighty nobly served with his servants, and very civil', and recorded that he was regarded as one of the best tennis players in England. Charles II apparently weighed himself after a game with Chicheley, to see how many pounds he had shed.[3] In 1686 Chicheley was to have been Warden of the Grocers' Company for the year, but the costs of high living, and possibly of building, had taken their toll. In that same year Chicheley was forced to sell the Wimpole estate, already encumbered with mortgages, for £51,000. The purchaser was his fellow Grocer Sir John Cutler, a colourful figure in the post-Restoration City and a principal benefactor of the Company. Cutler stood in for Chicheley as Warden (a post which eventually he held four times). Pepys's diary records many encounters with Cutler, including the outcry that ensued when it was discovered that Cutler had secured the Treasurership of the post-Fire St Paul's Cathedral by giving a donation of £1,500 to the repair fund. Cutler's way of life contrasted strongly with Chicheley's. Whereas Pepys thought Chicheley was

Sir Thomas Chicheley, the builder of the first Wimpole Hall, by William Dobson (private collection)

'a high flyer', it was said that Cutler was mean personally, but generous to others, that his 'habits of petty personal parsimony combine large benevolence and public spirit.'[4] Alexander Pope was to satirise Cutler's parsimony in his *Third Moral Essay*:

Cutler saw tenants break, and houses fall;
For very want he could not build a wall.
His only daughter in a stranger's power;
For very want he could not pay a dower.

For in 1689 Sir John Cutler's only child by his first marriage, Elizabeth, had married without her father's consent the 'stranger' Charles Robartes, who had recently become 2nd Earl of Radnor and was one of the principal supporters of the new king, William III. Only on his deathbed in 1693 did Cutler forgive his daughter, settling much of his valuable estate, including Wimpole, on Elizabeth, but within four years she was also dead. Radnor used her fortune to turn Wimpole into one of the great houses and gardens of the age of William and Mary, spending, it was said, some £20,000 in the process. Of the internal works which Radnor undoubtedly undertook there is now little trace, although some of the plasterwork in the coving of the Great Staircase has been dated to the late seventeenth century.

Sir Thomas Chicheley had previously enclosed a park around his new house and planted a great avenue to the south. Radnor was considerably more ambitious; he emparked the land as far as the eye could see in each direction, which probably entailed the demolition of the few surviving cottages within the new parkland. The features of the new design are all to be seen in the bird's-eye view by Leonard Knyff, engraved by John Kip in 1707. There are few vestiges of the great garden schemes that Radnor commissioned, which one contemporary advised were 'worth riding twenty miles out of the way to see'.[5]

Some parts of the scene engraved by Kip were not actually undertaken; but the great orangery to the west of the house was built, together with the service wing balancing it on the east, and a stable block at right angles overlooking the forecourt. The character of the design, the scale of the enterprise, and Radnor's connections at court, all point to the use of the royal gardeners George London and

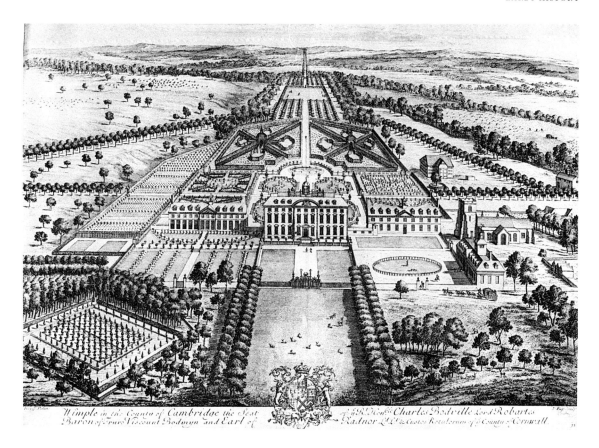

Bird's-eye view of the house and Lord Radnor's formal gardens in 1707; engraving by Leonard Knyff and John Kip

Henry Wise at Wimpole; and where London and Wise went, the maverick baroque architect William Talman, Comptroller of the King's Works, was rarely far behind. The orangery, with its bas-relief panels above the windows, has been attributed to Talman on stylistic grounds.

After all this effort, the financial strain proved too much for the Earl of Radnor. He had raised substantial sums by mortgaging the estate, and he was frequently unable to meet the interest payments on the debt. One of his leading lenders was his fellow-peer Lord Ashburnham, who used his banker Richard Hoare to press Radnor continually for payment. Financial circumstances forced Radnor to sell Wimpole in 1710 – a year when his political sympathies were becoming ever more Tory – and move back to the Robartes's family seat, Lan-

hydrock in Cornwall. The purchaser was John Holles, 1st Duke of Newcastle, who had only a short time to enjoy his new acquisition, for he died the following year in a riding accident, leaving his only child Henrietta Cavendish-Holles as principal heiress. Through her, Wimpole entered perhaps the most illustrious phase in its history.

NOTES

1 C.R.Elrington (ed.), *Victoria County History, Cambridgeshire [VCH]*, v (1973) pp.265–8; M. Spufford, *Contrasting communities: English villagers in the sixteenth and seventeenth centuries* (Cambridge, 1974), pp.xxiv–xxv.

2 W.M.Palmer (ed.), *John Layer of Shepreth*, Cambridgeshire Antiquarian Society, liii (1935), p.111

3 R.C.Latham and W.Matthews (eds), *The diary of Samuel Pepys*, viii, pp.418 9, ix, pp.112, *DNB*, DL, Add. MS 36228, fos 116, 124–8.

4 Op. cit., viii, p.85, iv, pp.22, 430; *DNB*.

5 Historical Manuscripts Commission [HMC], *Egmont MSS*, ii, p.206.

CHAPTER TWO

THE HARLEY YEARS (1711–40)

On 31 August 1713 the wedding took place in the drawing-room (probably what is now the Ante Room) at Wimpole Hall between Henrietta Cavendish-Holles and Edward, Lord Harley. There were few guests and little pomp, but this was intended to be one of the grand alliances of the reign of Queen Anne, for Lord Harley's father was the great Tory chief minister Robert Harley, 1st Earl of Oxford and Mortimer. It was a match for love as well as wealth and politics, one which had been speculated about for two years or more, and Lord Oxford's correspondents lost no time in guessing from his secrecy what might be afoot. 'We all agree', the other great politician of the day – and Oxford's rival – Bolingbroke wrote, 'that you have played, least in sight, as if you went to get a mistress for yourself instead of a wife for your son.'[1]

Political intriguers lost no time either, using Oxford's absence from London at his son's wedding as an opportunity to begin the process of bringing down the Tory oligarchy which had ruled throughout Queen Anne's reign. Oxford was to be the chief victim. 'His greatest fault', one of his contemporaries wrote later, 'was vanity; and his friendship was never to be depended upon, if it interfered with his other designs, though the sacrifice was to an enemy.'[2] As the ailing, childless Queen approached death and the prospect of Hanoverian (and Whiggish) kings grew nearer, so the intrigue among his opponents widened and became more open. Daniel Defoe, Lord Oxford's spy, reported that 'Your Lordship has but one way left with these men. They must be conquered; or the nation is undone, the Queen undone, and all Her Majesty's faithful friends and servants sacrificed to a raging and merciless party.' Finally the storm broke, and raging and merciless it proved to be.[3]

Oxford was stripped of his office of Lord High Treasurer in July 1714, was arrested on charges

of high treason in July 1715 and imprisoned in the Tower for two years. With the accession of George I at Queen Anne's death in August 1714, the Tories had been truly dished, and had to wait out the Whig hegemony for many political generations. Wimpole was to have become the national centre of Toryism triumphant; instead it embodied Toryism defiant.

The political background is crucial to understanding the history of Wimpole during the years of Harley ownership, when Edward, Lord Harley was revitalising it. Lord Harley inherited his father's title to become 2nd Earl of Oxford in 1724, but even before his wedding he had been planning the changes to Wimpole that were to make it one of the main centres of art and learning of the early Georgian age. The 1st Earl had been one of the great book collectors of his day; he employed the Anglo-Saxon scholar Humfrey Wanley to be his librarian, and together they assiduously collected a vast range of books and manuscripts that were of particular importance for writing England's history. The 2nd Earl inherited that collecting zeal – almost a mania – and quickly began to find ways of accommodating the fruits of their joint passion. Wimpole was intended to be the main location for the books the Harleys collected, as well as of the paintings and other antiquities that Edward Harley amassed, although space at Wimpole was at a premium, and probably a substantial part of the collection never left London. An ambitious new garden scheme swept away much of the design installed for Lord Radnor, and the interior of Wimpole Hall was transformed into one of the grandest baroque country houses in England.

In the 1710s the architect most favoured by the Tory grandees was the Scottish-born and Italian-educated James Gibbs. His rise to prominence was due in large part to Harley's patronage and to a

Edward Harley, 2nd Earl of Oxford; drawing by Michael Dahl, before 1719 (British Museum)

The Library, built by James Gibbs to house part of Edward Harley's vast book collection

circle of Harley friends and relations. It was through Harley that Gibbs obtained his first major commission, the new London church of St Mary-le-Strand, in 1713. In the same year Gibbs also began work both on his patron's London house and at Wimpole. Gibbs's first schemes for Wimpole may pre-date the Harley–Holles marriage; they seem to show the original house retained, but with a massive new library block added to it. This scheme was never executed, although its essence was retained. Gradually over nearly twenty years Gibbs's plans for Wimpole were realised. In addition to considerable internal redecoration, of which parts of the intricate plasterwork on the Great Staircase are the most

significant survival, Gibbs designed for Harley a sequence of rooms to house his books and other treasures on the west side of the house, and a grand chapel on the east.

So many changes have been wrought in the built fabric of Wimpole since Gibbs worked there that it is not always easy to identify the chronology of the Harley rooms. Fortunately, Harley and his circle were great correspondents, and letters survive that fill in many of the gaps. After a slow beginning, the result of both the 1st Lord Oxford's political disgrace and financial embarrassment, work seems to have been well under way by 1716. Meanwhile Lady Harley was engaged in a protracted dispute over the inheritance of her father, the Duke of Newcastle's, estate, which was only resolved in 1719, when she received a reduced portion.

In 1716, Harley wrote to Humfrey Wanley, 'You will be wanted at Wimpole, now the room for my books is finished, to put them up and catalogue.' On 30 November Wanley wrote back that the book room 'looks with an uncommon and grand air' with its two-feet-long green tasselled strings on the bookcases, and Wanley also mentioned books in 'the Lesser Room'.[4] The library grew at an astonishing rate, with some 12,000 books in the collection by September 1717. Work on the next phase of the library began in the following summer. Dr Covel, Master of Christ's College, Cambridge, whose library Harley was desperate to acquire, reported in August 1718 that Harley was 'building and furnishing a Vatican' at Wimpole. The following June

Wanley wrote that 'within a few weeks I hope to be at Wimpole, where His Lordship hath lately built five large rooms for a Library, which I hope to fill this summer, with as choice a parcel of books as any in England.' By May 1720 guests were being admitted to these new library rooms.[5]

The first library that Gibbs built at Wimpole was almost certainly in parts of what are now the South Drawing Room, the Gallery and the Book Room. Much of it seems to have been in a state of half-ordered muddle, to judge by the instructions and comments that passed to and fro. The Harley library was even to receive books in bequests from grateful bibliophiles containing volumes that those enthusiasts had previously pilfered on visits to Wimpole.

The Chapel, built by Gibbs and decorated with illusionistic murals by Sir James Thornhill. The service books are all that remain at Wimpole of the Harleian Library

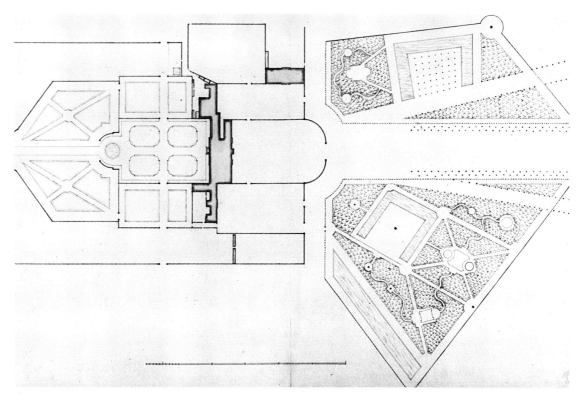

Bridgeman's design for planting the South Avenue, c.1720. Lord Radnor's formal parterres are shown to the north of the house

Eventually, as the collection grew ever larger, these rooms proved insufficient for their task, and the present Library was built, as a grand extension to the main house.

Gibbs designed the large double-cube room for his patron, by now Earl of Oxford, which would contain the bulk of the book collection. Accounts suggest that in 1728 the book presses were being moved in (although no longer under Wanley's supervision, for he died in 1726), and by 1730 the extension seems to have been largely complete. Workmen were, however, still being paid for roofing in 1732. The Great Library was built at much the same time as Gibbs was undertaking the Senate House building for the University of Cambridge, a commission that also came through the good offices of the Earl of Oxford, who had become High Steward of the University in 1726. The

Library plasterwork ceiling bears some resemblance to the Senate House scheme, attributed to Giovanni Bagutti and Isaac Mansfield, who may therefore have worked at Wimpole as well.

Balancing the western extension of the original house, Gibbs designed a chapel for Harley on the east, with a grand pew for the family in the gallery approached from the Entrance Hall and Ante-Chapel, while the main body of the Chapel was entered from basement level. Gibbs's original ornate plans for a building whose internal wall surfaces were to be modelled, and ornamented with sculpture, were superseded by what is essentially a brick box five bays long, inside which the baroque magic of Sir James Thornhill's *trompe l'oeil* painting was allowed free rein. It is one of the crowning works in Thornhill's career, a career that was fast declining by the time of the Wimpole commission as taste was abandoning such illusions. Although the chapel was largely complete by 1724, the music that the resident musician Thomas Tudway had composed for the consecration of Lord Oxford's chapel was not performed, for the service was apparently never held. It was doubtless one of the victims of the financial difficulties that were already beginning to beset the Harley estates.

Thornhill also painted scenes inside the summer-houses that Gibbs built for the new gardens at Wimpole, and the classical urns inside the Chapel were echoed by Gibbs's designs for urns and busts to adorn the north gardens. At the same time, Harley commissioned the garden designer Charles Bridgeman to implement new schemes for the Wimpole landscape. The old gardens were swept away or incorporated into new, formal designs. Between about 1720 and 1725 Bridgeman and his workmen planned, felled, dug and planted. The grandest part of the entire design was the great South Avenue of elms, extending for well over 2 miles with a central vista 90 yards wide; the avenue crossed the Cambridge road where it spread out to encircle an octagonal basin fed by the River Cam. It terminated in a wood some way to the south. In all, this scheme incorporated 1,216 trees; the avenue survived until Dutch elm disease struck in the 1970s.

Library, chapel, gardens: Gibbs, Thornhill and Bridgeman had transformed the interior and sur-roundings of Wimpole for their patron, although as one correspondent noted, the 'house does not appear to be very modern on the outside'. Rather, 'the rooms inside are very handsome', for Harley employed a galaxy of talent to adorn the interiors. When Gibbs's Great Library was nearing comple-tion, Alexander Pope wrote with great expecta-tions. 'I am impatient to . . . see what fine new lodgings the Ancients are to have? I salute the little gods and antiquities in my way in the ante-room, wishing them joy of the new temples they are to be enshrined in . . .'[6] Ancient sculptures rubbed shoulders with new works by Michael Rysbrack, another artist brought to prominence by Harley. Portraits of the Stuart kings and queens, of great collectors, and of all Harley's artistic and political friends, many painted by Michael Dahl, an artist much favoured by the Tories, looked down from the walls of the first-floor gallery and of the drawing-rooms. Every available space was filled by hunting scenes and the portraits of horses and other

This preparatory sketch by Thornhill shows five of the leading figures in Harley's circle: (from left to right) his portrait painter, Michael Dahl, his decorative painter, James Thornhill, his animal painter, John Wootton, his architect, James Gibbs, and his librarian, Humfrey Wanley (Art Institute of Chicago)

animals like the antelope from Harley's menageries and his wife's pet dog Casey seated on a cushion, by the great sporting artist John Wootton. Cabinets held treasures, curiosities and coins. Books seemed to be stored everywhere. Wimpole was filled with one of the greatest collections of its day, or indeed of any day.

The ensemble of people and objects that Harley drew together at Wimpole was of political as well as artistic significance. It should never be forgotten that the Harleys were effectively in the political wilderness from the end of Queen Anne's reign. The interiors at Wimpole, of which the Chapel is the finest surviving example, were a late flowering of the English baroque. Harley surrounded himself with men of similar Tory outlook. Pope and Swift, the greatest literary figures of the day, were frequent visitors to Wimpole. Harley was the patron and great protector of another Tory, the poet and former diplomat Matthew Prior, who died at Wimpole in 1721. Harley's daughter, the 'noble lovely little Peggy', said of Prior that he 'made himself beloved by every living thing in the house – master, child and servant, human creature or animal.' The engraver George Vertue, whose notebooks are one of the most important sources of information on art and artists in these years, was Harley's companion at home and on his travels. Harley paid for Francis Bird's monument to his father-in-law, the Duke of Newcastle, which set a new canon for sculpture in Westminster Abbey. There is a strong case for arguing that Harley was trying to establish an alternative, Tory artistic group around Wimpole, his London home in Dover Street, and on the great London estate he was building north of Oxford Street. Gibbs, Bridgeman and Wootton all took leases on houses on the estate, as did several Tory grandees. The street names of the area still recall the family and its allies: Harley, Wimpole, Henrietta, Holles, Cavendish, Queen Anne. Plans for the estate included a projected great library building where ultimately the whole Harley collection would have been housed.

Around 1720 Harley helped found the Virtuosi of St Luke, a club whose members mainly enjoyed his patronage. They toasted him at their meetings as 'one of the noble encouragers of arts and sciences,

painting and sculpture especially, in England.' It was certainly fun being in the Harley circle: Humfrey Wanley's letters from Wimpole are filled with stories of pranks, and when Thornhill, Bridgeman, Gibbs and Wootton went to see progress on the work at Wimpole in March 1721, their journey was immortalised in Thornhill's comic poem 'A hue and cry':

. . . Well since they're got thither, then there let
  'em stay
I'm sure they'll be welcome on every day
There's all things in plenty that Heart can desire
Fish, Flesh, & good Fowl, in each room a Fire.

Ambrosia's there, & delicate nectar,
But to Crown all the rest, OF ARTS, a PROTECTOR;
Surrounded with Pickaxes, mattocks, & spade
The Ballad is ended, in wheelbarrow made.[7]

The collections that Harley and his father amassed were intended, at least in part, to be the source materials for a great history of the English people; and the Harleian manuscripts (which were kept mainly at the Harley London home) remain one of the most important collections on the subject. The design of the new buildings at Wimpole also formed part of the scheme. When originally built, the Great Library had windows only in the east wall, facing the light of dawn. The representation of the Doctors of the Church in the Chapel's painted decoration, like the similar scheme which Thornhill executed for All Souls College, Oxford, was an expression of great learning as well as piety. Building a chapel was itself an expression of High Church Toryism: some Whig houses, like Sir Robert Walpole's Houghton in Norfolk, had no chapel. The works of art with which Harley surrounded himself spoke of an English tradition and of Tory defiance.

The Whig grandees like the Duke of Chandos at his magnificent Middlesex house, Canons, and the artistic and architectural avant garde behind Lord Burlington, cultivated styles that were essentially foreign: the music of Handel, the art of Italy and France, buildings in the style of Palladio. James Gibbs may have owed his early success to Tory patronage, but he was too shrewd a businessman and intelligent an artist not to realise that the future lay with Palladianism. Certainly he had a hand in

Colen Campbell's design for Walpole's Houghton, one of the quintessential buildings in the new Palladian style, which Harley hated when he saw it on one of his many travels. He thought it 'neither magnificent nor beautiful, there is a very great expense without either judgement or taste.'[8]

Yet by the 1730s it was Harley who seemed increasingly out of step: the third edition (1742) of Daniel Defoe's *Tour through the whole island of Great Britain*, which had been so complimentary about Wimpole before, now said that the estate was 'situated in a very dirty country, and notwithstanding the cost bestowed upon it from its first owner to this time, the gardens and buildings are both in a very bad taste.' Whereas in the 1720s activity was continuing on all fronts, not only at Wimpole but also on his London estate, by the 1730s Harley's great building programme was almost entirely at an end. The last significant work at Wimpole was the restoration in 1732 of the north chapel, containing the Chicheley family tombs, in Wimpole's medieval parish church, intended in due course to become the Harley family's final resting-place. Activity still continued in one area, the acquisition of books and manuscripts, often at considerably inflated prices.

Those who benefited from Harley patronage were unstinting in their praise. Zachary Grey's memoir described Lord Oxford as 'indeed rich, but thankful; charitable without ostentation; and that in so good-natured a way as never to give pain to the persons whom he obliged in that respect.'[9] Other verdicts were harsher. As a Tory he was excluded from office, but he seems in any case to have suffered from political inertia, taking refuge in his collecting from the political as well as the financial realities around him. He also took refuge in drink. His wife's fortune proved insufficient to maintain his expensive style, and a crisis was finally reached in 1739. On 4 November Wimpole and its landed estate, already heavily mortgaged, were sold for £86,740 to one of the most successful Whig luminaries, Lord Hardwicke, the Lord Chancellor. The sale agreements make poignant reading. Lord Oxford was to remain at Wimpole until Midsummer 1740, during which time he was to remove all his books and furnishings, although if the books

from the Great Library could not be removed in time, they might remain until Lady Day 1741. Toryism defiant became Toryism dejected, and the Harleys moved out.

Mrs Delany wrote that Lord Oxford 'has of late been so entirely given up to drinking, that his life has been no pleasure to him or satisfaction to his friends . . . He has had no enjoyment of the world since his mismanagement of his affairs; it has hurt his body and mind, and *hastened his death*.'[10] For within a short space of time, on 16 June 1741, Lord Oxford was dead. Lady Mary Wortley Montagu recorded that he had advanced his death 'by choice, refusing all remedies till it was too late to make use of them. There was a will found dated 1728 in which he gave everything to my Lady, which has affected her very much, notwithstanding the many reasons she has had to complain of him. I always thought

The frontispiece to the catalogue for the 1741 sale of Lord Oxford's collection, engraved by his friend and travelling companion, the connoisseur George Vertue

17

there was more weakness than dishonesty in his actions . . .'[11]

A sale of the works of art and curiosities that Harley had collected took six days from 8 March 1742. An Egyptian blowing-horn, two knives, and a Turkish general's truncheon fetched £3 4s, ten old portrait heads a guinea, Van Dyck's Digby family group £173 5s, Dahl's portrait of Gibbs £1 12s, Dobson's portrait of 'Mr Chicheley's head with a band' £3 5s . . . The widowed Countess kept back a number of items, especially the great Wootton horse pictures; they descended through the Dukes of Portland, since Lord Oxford's heiress and only daughter Margaret married the 2nd Duke of Portland in 1734.

The book collection was the next to go; Lady Oxford sold it for only £13,000 in 1744 – a price which was lower than even the binding cost of the

Ivory bust by David Le Marchard of Lord Somers in the Library, where many of his books are now preserved. Owned by Lord Oxford and the 1st Earl of Hardwicke, it left Wimpole in 1940, but has now returned at the wish of Prof. Sir Albert Richardson's family

volumes. By the end of Oxford's life it had grown to 50,000 printed books, 41,000 prints and 350,000 pamphlets. The manuscript collection, which had always been intended as a foundation for a great British Library, was acquired for the nation in 1753, again at a bargain price: £10,000 bought the 7,639 manuscript volumes and 14,236 rolls. Very little remains at Wimpole, other than the buildings and traces of the garden, to show what was once there. A few bound service books in the Chapel are the sole remnants of the Harleian Library.

That Lord Oxford was still collecting omnivorously even up to the point of the crash is evident in his acquisition of some of the manuscripts of Lord Somers, the Whig Chancellor in the last years of the seventeenth century. Somers may have been a political opponent, but he was nevertheless an important collector. To celebrate his purchase, Oxford bought an ivory bust of Lord Somers that was to join the pantheon in the Wimpole library. Lord Hardwicke – Somers's nephew-in-law – bought the bust, which is one of the Huguenot ivory carver David Le Marchand's masterpieces, at the sale of 1742. Now it sits in Lord Harley's Library as a tangible reminder of the transfer of ownership and family to the Earls of Hardwicke.

NOTES

1 HMC, *Portland MSS*, v, p.325.

2 Lord Dartmouth's footnote to Bishop Burnet, *History of his own time*, 6 vol. ed. (Oxford, 1833), vi, p.50.

3 G.H.Healey (ed.), *The letters of Daniel Defoe* (Oxford, 1955), p.432.

4 P.L.Heyworth (ed.), *The letters of Humfrey Wanley* (Oxford 1989), p.361.

5 HMC, *Portland MSS*, v, p.562; Heyworth (ed.), *Letters of Humfrey Wanley*, p.396.

6 G.Sherburn (ed.), *The Correspondence of Alexander Pope*, iii (1956), p.114.

7 *Wren Society*, xvii (1940), pp.12–13.

8 HMC, *Portland MSS*, vi, p.160.

9 BL, Add MS 5834, fo. 162.

10 Lady Llanover (ed.), *The autobiography and correspondence of Mrs Delany*, 6 vols (1861–2), ii, p.156.

11 R.Halsband (ed.), *The complete letters of Lady Mary Wortley Montagu*, 3 vols (Oxford, 1966–7), ii, pp.246–7.

CHAPTER THREE

THE 1ST AND 2ND EARLS OF HARDWICKE (1740–90)

Although Lord Hardwicke shared some of the attributes of the man from whom he purchased Wimpole, notably an abiding interest in books, he was in most ways entirely different from Lord Oxford. He had a superfluity of sons (unlike Harley who was survived only by a daughter), and one of the most extraordinary political and judicial careers of the eighteenth century. The acquisition of Wimpole proved to be one of his greatest joys.

Philip Yorke was born at Dover in 1690, son of an attorney but otherwise of relatively undistinguished birth. (He had connections within the landed gentry, however: the Yorkes of Erddig were descended from his cousin.) Yorke's inexorable rise began after he was called to the Bar in 1714, the year of the political eclipse of the Tory Harleys. In succession he was an MP from 1718, Solicitor-General with a knighthood in 1720, when he was the youngest counsel on the western circuit, Attorney-General in 1724, and Lord Chief Justice of King's Bench in 1733, when he was made a baron. (His title came from the Gloucestershire estate of Hardwicke which he had bought in 1725.) He was given the Great Seal as Lord Chancellor in 1737, and finally an earldom in 1754, two years before he resigned as one of the longest-serving of all Lord Chancellors. It is said that George II did not recognise Lord Hardwicke at court after he left office, since the king had never seen him without his robes of state and full wig.[1] As Lord Chancellor, he was pre-eminent in shaping the law of equity; some of the legislation he framed still affects our lives, notably his Marriage Act of 1754 which established the legal basis for the conduct and definition of marriages in England and Wales. Lord Hardwicke was a loyal Whig, and he remained a political force until very shortly before his death in 1764.

Opinions of Lord Hardwicke were divided – usually along political lines – and there is little doubt that a wish to cement his own and his family's position in political and polite society was a lifetime's ambition. Contemporaries piled one story about Hardwicke meanness upon another. Horace Walpole in 1762 complained of the 'miserable and pernicious turn of the whole family, than which nothing can be more illiberal and wretched, though possessed of immense wealth and the children matched into the most wealthy families' – with expectations, he added, that the wealth would ultimately revert to the Yorkes.[2]

The family letters seem to tell quite a different

Philip, 1st Earl of Hardwicke, Lord Chancellor, who acquired Wimpole in 1740; painting from the studio of Michael Dahl (National Portrait Gallery)

THE YORKE FAMILY

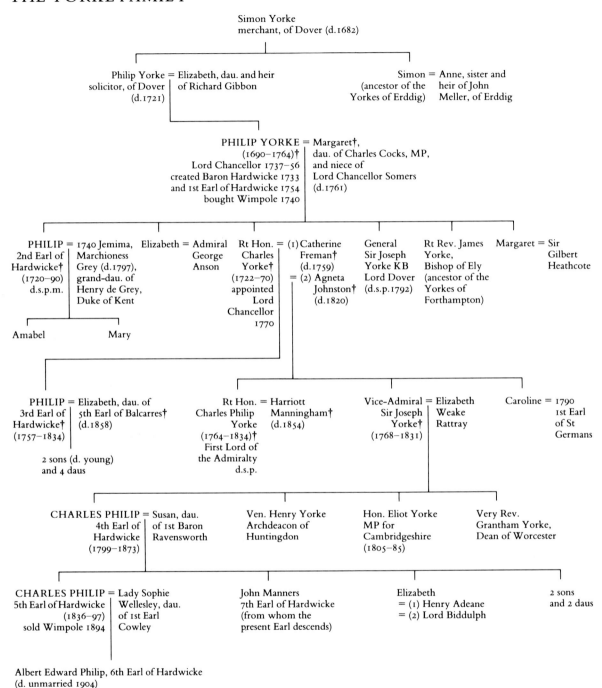

Simon Yorke
merchant, of Dover (d.1682)

Philip Yorke = Elizabeth, dau. and heir
solicitor, of Dover | of Richard Gibbon
(d.1721)

Simon = Anne, sister and
(ancestor of the | heir of John
Yorkes of Erddig) | Meller, of Erddig

PHILIP YORKE = Margaret†,
(1690–1764)† | dau. of Charles Cocks, MP,
Lord Chancellor 1737–56 | and niece of
created Baron Hardwicke 1733 | Lord Chancellor Somers
and 1st Earl of Hardwicke 1754 | (d.1761)
bought Wimpole 1740

PHILIP = 1740 Jemima,
2nd Earl of | Marchioness
Hardwicke† | Grey (d.1797),
(1720–90) | grand-dau. of
d.s.p.m. | Henry de Grey,
Duke of Kent

Elizabeth = Admiral
George
Anson

Rt Hon. = (1) Catherine
Charles | Fremant†
Yorke† | (d.1759)
(1722–70) | = (2) Agneta
appointed | Johnston†
Lord | (d.1820)
Chancellor
1770

General
Sir Joseph
Yorke KB
Lord Dover
(d.s.p.1792)

Rt Rev. James
Yorke,
Bishop of Ely
(ancestor of the
Yorkes of
Forthampton)

Margaret = Sir
Gilbert
Heathcote

Amabel   Mary

PHILIP = Elizabeth, dau. of
3rd Earl of | 5th Earl of Balcarres†
Hardwicke† | (d.1858)
(1757–1834)

2 sons (d. young)
and 4 daus

Rt Hon. = Harriott
Charles Philip | Manningham†
Yorke | (d.1854)
(1764–1834)†
First Lord of
the Admiralty
d.s.p.

Vice-Admiral = Elizabeth
Sir Joseph | Weake
Yorke† | Rattray
(1768–1831)

Caroline = 1790
1st Earl
of St
Germans

CHARLES PHILIP = Susan, dau.
4th Earl of | of 1st Baron
Hardwicke | Ravensworth
(1799–1873)

Ven. Henry Yorke
Archdeacon of
Huntingdon

Hon. Eliot Yorke
MP for
Cambridgeshire
(1805–85)

Very Rev.
Grantham Yorke,
Dean of Worcester

CHARLES PHILIP = Lady Sophie
5th Earl of Hardwicke | Wellesley, dau.
(1836–97) | of 1st Earl
sold Wimpole 1894 | Cowley

John Manners
7th Earl of Hardwicke
(from whom the
present Earl descends)

Elizabeth
= (1) Henry Adeane
= (2) Lord Biddulph

2 sons
and 2 daus

Albert Edward Philip, 6th Earl of Hardwicke
(d. unmarried 1904)

Owners of Wimpole are set in CAPITALS   †indicates monument in Wimpole Church

story, in which the Lord Chancellor and his wife – the niece of Lord Chancellor Somers, whose ivory bust had been one of the last additions to the adornments of the Harley Library – revelled in the company of their growing family, especially in the late summer when everyone congregated at Wimpole. 'Let us know when you fix your day to come to us,' the Lord Chancellor wrote to his eldest son in 1747, 'which we very much long for' – although business was usually mixed with pleasure: 'Don't forget to bring with you the accounts and papers relating to the election that we may settle that affair.' Philip Yorke's display of filial piety in return was touching, for he was 'impatient to throw myself at your feet at Wimpole, and hope to find you with as much health and spirits as the country never fails to give you.'[3]

Soon after Lord Hardwicke acquired Wimpole in 1740, and wishing to put the house to family rather than scholarly use, he began substantial works which recast the exterior into its present appearance. Whereas Harley as a Tory had patronised James Gibbs, Hardwicke chose as his architect Henry Flitcroft, who had risen from humble beginnings through the patronage and influence of the 3rd Earl of Burlington. It is said that Flitcroft came to the attention of the noble architect when he fell off scaffolding and broke his leg while working as a journeyman carpenter on Burlington House in 1720, and during his recuperation Burlington spotted his fine drawing skills. Flitcroft was to be known

thereafter as 'Burlington Harry'. Whig private patrons proved to be the mainstay of his practice, right up to his last works, the great garden buildings at Stourhead of the 1750s and '60s for the Hoares.

When Lord Hardwicke acquired Wimpole it was externally a mixture of styles: the mid-seventeenth-century Chicheley house, the late Stuart orangery, and Gibbs's wings and library. The survey drawings Flitcroft made of the exterior show how jumbled it had become, and he gave Wimpole a homogeneous face, rebuilding both north and south fronts in red brick with Portland stone dressings. In place of the projecting central and end bays of Chicheley's house, Flitcroft's southern façade is all on one plane, though with the middle three bays brought forward very slightly, and emphasised by a broad pediment containing the arms and coronet of Baron Hardwicke (as he then was). The only consciously Palladian features occur in the very centre, with the Venetian window, the semi-circular Diocletian window above it, and the boldly rusticated portal below, approached by a balustraded double staircase. He also placed a bow window on each main floor in the centre of the partly rebuilt north, or garden, front. The result was a more fashionable and elegant, but also more severe, façade that must have appealed to Lord Hardwicke.

Inside, Harley's cabinet rooms were thrown into one to make a ground-floor gallery at the west end of the house for Lord Hardwicke's famous picture collection, which included works by Rubens, Hol-

Flitcroft's design for refacing the south front, made in 1742

bein, Cuyp and Titian. Columns mark where the former dividing walls had been. Otherwise, new work largely consisted of grandiose decoration. The carver Sefferin Alken added the chimney-pieces in the Gallery and in the remodelled Saloon in the centre of the garden front. The plasterer Thomas Betson provided the decorative stucco work in collaboration with Giuseppe Artari. Matthias Lock seems to have supplied new furniture.

Flitcroft's own schedule of works shows the delicacy of the task and the attention to detail of an architect who had begun his working life as a craftsman. The work for the carpenter (whom the accounts reveal to have been a Mr Ratford) was itemised:

To shore up the several floors while the alterations are making and front is rebuilding; to make all the naked flooring, quartered partitioning, according to the plans; to make a new back staircase, in which to employ as much of the old as will come in . . . to frame a good trussed roof and a ceiling floor to the attic storey, and prepare the timber work for the skylight over the back stairs, and to make a balustrade and a new cupola, and to repair the floor and boarding of the flats, to make new guttering to the outer and inner gutter.[4]

The schedule suggests that Lord Hardwicke's famed financial tightness may have been responsible for some of these instructions, where existing work was improved upon or repaired, like the roof and the lightwell, rather than replaced wholesale. The instructions to John Jones the painter are more terse, so cannot be used to verify one of the many stories that circulated about the Hardwickes' meanness. 'My Lord', one contemporary (and Tory) critic wrote, 'was for having [a sitting room] an ash or olive colour as being the cheaper and more durable. But my Lady objected that, although more expensive, the fashionable French white would be cheaper in the end' – it enabled two candles to light the room rather than four.[5]

Some £7,000 was spent on Flitcroft's works between 1742 and 1745, and the architect seems to have done occasional work for the Hardwickes for another ten years (as well as working for their eldest son and his wife at Wrest, in Bedfordshire). The Library gained in light with the addition of a bay

window in its north, end wall. Although the idea for it was claimed by the Warwickshire gentleman-architect Sanderson Miller,[6] this too seems more likely to have been a Flitcroft job, judging by the carved decoration of swags and lion masks around the bay which matches that known to be by Sefferin Alken in the Saloon. Flitcroft also undertook the almost total rebuilding of Wimpole parish church for Lord Hardwicke (see Chapter Nine). The plans for the church were delivered in February 1748, and a price of £1,058 was agreed a month later when work started.

While work was proceeding on the house and church, little attention was paid to the gardens. The travelling antiquarian William Stukeley visited Wimpole in October 1747, and his sketches of the north garden and grand avenue show only minor remodelling of the entrance court and the parterres of Bridgeman's schemes, modifications probably carried out by the Wimpole gardeners.[7] Within a few years the park and gardens were beginning the process of transformation into the landscaped design more familiar to us today.

By 1753 Jemima, Marchioness Grey, Lord Hardwicke's daughter-in-law, was able to write, in a letter to her friend Mary Talbot, the perfect description of the new arrangements:

I have found here quite a new place, my Lord having now completed his gardens, and nothing ever made a greater change or a more different scene. Instead of straight gravel walks with borders and cross plots surrounded by walls, and views into the park through iron gates, there is now a large green lawn behind the house, bounded by clumps of trees and flowering shrubs, a broad serpentine walk through them, and enclosed with a sunk fence that lets the park quite into the garden.[8]

Novel schemes like this were gaining acceptance in the 1750s; one name associated with them is that of William Shenstone, gentleman-gardener of The Leasowes in Worcestershire, who in printed instruction and his own garden planning combined artifice and nature, especially in constructing serpentine walks with strategically planned views. Shenstone may have been the otherwise anonymous 'Mr S.' who wrote to Lord Hardwicke in 1752 with 'Hints about alterations in the garden'. The suggestions

Jemima, Marchioness Grey, by Allan Ramsay, 1741 (Gallery). In 1740 she married Philip Yorke, later 2nd Earl of Hardwicke

The carved wooden chimney-piece and overmantel in the South Drawing Room were designed by Flitcroft in the 1740s

Design by Sanderson Miller for the Gothic Tower

were similar to those actually implemented by Lord Hardwicke, using the services of the son of the Royal gardener, Robert Greening. Some of the formal elements in the garden were removed, notably the north garden where Gibbs's summer-houses with their Thornhill-painted interiors were destroyed, new serpentine walks made, and ha-has were dug to make a barrier the park animals could not cross. The old avenues had trees strategically removed 'to form the horse chestnuts into clumps, so as to open the view up the side of the hill from the house and garden'.[9]

Sanderson Miller, the Warwickshire antiquarian and designer who was a neighbour and friend of William Shenstone, designed an eye-catching folly tower with crumbling battlements and delicate Gothic traceried windows for the hill due north of the house at Wimpole. It was an early example of the revival of interest in Gothic architecture, and was based on Miller's Gothic tower at Hagley in Worcestershire, built in 1747 In 1749, George Lyttelton, the owner of Hagley, advised Miller that Lord Hardwicke was considering a similar tower, but he 'wants no house or even room in it, but merely the walls and semblence of an old castle to make an object for his house'. Miller obliged. In

February 1751, when he submitted an amended design, he urged Lord Hardwicke to begin work soon. The cautious Lord Chancellor decided not to proceed – he felt the castle should remain in the air a little longer – and the designs waited another twenty years to be implemented.[10] The garden scheme he had commissioned proved delightful enough for him and his family: Marchioness Grey described the outlook beyond the ha-ha where the deer fed and the sheep grazed, tended by a boy who sang all day long and who tried, usually to no avail, to catch birds on limed twigs.[11]

By the time of his death in 1764, Lord Hardwicke could survey his own and his family's achievements with justifiable pride. In 1740, the year he moved into Wimpole, his heir Philip Yorke had married Jemima, Marchioness Grey, grand-daughter of the Duke of Kent and entitled by special remainder to bear a title in her own right; Lord Hardwicke was especially fond of their daughters Amabel and Mary. Philip Yorke had a safe and undistinguished career in the House of Commons as MP for Reigate and then Cambridgeshire, but real advancement was reserved for Lord Hardwicke's second son Charles, whom he lived to see become Attorney-General, and prominent in 1762 and 1763 in the

25

official stand against the populist sedition of John Wilkes and his *North Briton* newspaper. Of the younger sons Joseph became a career diplomat, James a clergyman and eventually Bishop of Ely, and John a lawyer and politician; Hardwicke's daughter Elizabeth married Admiral Anson, the naval hero who circled the globe and amassed the treasure which enabled his brother to build the Staffordshire house of Shugborough, and the youngest child Margaret married the wealthy Sir Gilbert Heathcote. 'It would give you a real and heartfelt delight . . .', the Marchioness Grey wrote, 'to hear Lord H–ke talk every day of *his Congress* filling; nor should I omit to mention with gratitude his goodness to my children, who will be out of their little wits when all their friends are here together.' It was the work he had undertaken at Wimpole of which Lord Hardwicke was particu-

The tomb of Lord Chancellor Hardwicke in the Chicheley chapel

larly proud. 'You are very obliging to speak so handsomely of Wimpole . . . it would give me much pleasure to be convinced that you really like it', he wrote to his son Philip in 1757. 'I made it for you, and hope to leave it to you with comfort.'[12]

Comfort was one thing Lord Hardwicke did not have when he died on 6 March 1764 at the age of 74, with severe intestinal pains; the memorial he desired to have built at Wimpole for himself and his recently deceased wife was to be 'decent but not magnificent, and the inscription modest'.[13] Within a few months the new, 2nd Earl of Hardwicke had erected a grandiose monument to his parents within the Chicheley chapel at Wimpole, employing James 'Athenian' Stuart, who was working for the Ansons at Shugborough, to design it, with Peter Schee-makers as the sculptor. The inscription on the Lord Chancellor's monument was somewhat less modest than its dedicatee had instructed, and the design extolled virtues as much as did the words. As Stuart wrote to Thomas Anson, 'on one side is Minerva, not the warlike but the eloquent, and therefore instead of the lance she holds a caduceus [the rod of Hermes] . . . On the other side is Pudicitia, the matronal virtue. She is veiled and holds a stem of lilies . . . of the two middle-most [children] one collects the Mace and Purse [of the Lord Chancellor] and the other crowns it with a garland.'[14]

The new Earl was considerably more interested in books and manuscripts than in the rough and tumble of political life, and he consistently refused high office. He and his brother Charles had had an extraordinary undergraduate career at Cambridge, where they and other friends and fellow-students had published the supposed correspondence of an agent of the King of Persia residing at Athens during the Peloponnesian War (in a limited edition), which enjoyed surprising success throughout the rest of the century. Both brothers remained keen students of old documents, dedicated to their preservation – although Charles, when working on the manuscripts of his great-uncle Lord Somers in 1752, managed to destroy most of them and burn down his house at Lincoln's Inn when he knocked a candle over. Philip, both before his inheritance and after, collected State Papers, especially those of the late sixteenth and early seventeenth centuries, which he

The 2nd Earl of Hardwicke, by Gainsborough (private collection)

eventually published in a great series of volumes.

As chairman of the parliamentary committee which paved the way for the establishment of the British Museum in 1753, the 2nd Earl was intimately involved with the acquisition for the nation of the Harleian Manuscripts, part of the great collection of the Earls of Oxford. His high regard for Sir Robert Walpole also led to the publication in 1781 of his collection of *Walpoliana*, a subject which his family grew to dread as the collector was apt to expand on his hero at the slightest opportunity. Together with the Earl of Dartmouth and Speaker Onslow, Hardwicke also undertook an annotated edition of Bishop Gilbert Burnet's *History of my own times*. Burnet was a particular favourite of William of Orange, espousing his claim to the throne with a Whig partisanship that disgusted the Tory Harleys – the 2nd Earl of Oxford's uncle described it as 'the most false, partial and imperfect work of the kind I ever read'.[15] Burnet's portrait, an enormous canvas by Sir Godfrey Kneller, was the central painting in

the Great Library at Wimpole, and it still hangs in the house, the only major picture to have remained from the time of the Hardwickes.

So Wimpole again became the centre of a great book and manuscript collection, as the 2nd Earl filled the Library, building upon the substantial legal and historical collection of his father. Little work was undertaken on the house, with the exception of the construction in 1777-8 of the Eating Room, the grand state dining-room built by Kenton Couse (Flitcroft's former assistant) in the north-east corner of the house. Couse probably also oversaw redecoration of bedrooms on the first floor at about the same time (when the State Bed seems to have been moved upstairs from the Saloon), and then alterations to the east kitchen block in the later 1780s. New furnishings were supplied by Thomas Chippendale & Co. in the years after 1777, and the Hardwickes commissioned paintings, especially from Angelica Kauffmann and Sir Joshua Reynolds. Reynolds's portrait of their two daughters, Amabel and Mary, with a dog (now in the Cleveland Museum of Art) is particularly charming. When Lord Hardwicke's niece Elizabeth Yorke (later Countess of St Germans) visited Wimpole in 1781, she found it a mixture of the new and the old-fashioned:

Most part of it is furnished in the old style, as for example Mama's and my apartment are brown wainscots, and the bed-curtains and hangings are crimson damask laced with gold most dreadfully tarnished. The rooms below stairs are excellent, and very handsomely furnished. Lady Grey, the Marchioness, has just fitted up some new apartments, that are beautiful, particularly the new dining room, which is very elegant indeed.

The household followed a rather rigid daily household routine – of which another visitor said, 'Nothing can be more polite than my entertainment at Wimpole has been. The economy is too steady, or has too much sameness, to please for a long time together.'[16] To escape, Elizabeth Yorke would 'always take a walk in the garden before breakfast', and it was in the grounds that her uncle left his most effective mark upon Wimpole.

At Wrest, six years before Lord Chancellor Hardwicke died, his heir and Marchioness Grey had

27

begun patronising the most promising rising star of the gardening world, Lancelot 'Capability' Brown. His landscaping skills were introduced to Wimpole in 1769. Marchioness Grey was exhilarated: 'Mr Brown has been leading me such a fairy circle and his magic wand has raised such landscapes to the eye – not visionary for they were all there but his touch has brought them out with the same effect as a painter's pencil upon canvas – that after having hobbled over rough ground to points that I had never seen before, for two hours, I return half-tired and half-footsore . . .'[17]

Brown's principal contribution to the Wimpole landscape was a wider extension of the park (taking in previously cultivated fields on the western, Arrington side) with belts of trees on the margins of the park, the further destruction of the old formal avenues, introducing characteristic clumps of trees in open ground, and a new lake. Beyond that the folly tower which Sanderson Miller had proposed to the 1st Earl was finally constructed on Johnson's Hill, reached across a wooden 'Chinese' bridge. Brown had Miller's original sketch design for the ruin adapted for greater historical accuracy, probably by the Cambridge architect James Essex. 'Athenian' Stuart came back to Wimpole to design a two-storey 'Prospect House' (now gone) on a rise in the west of the park.

Lord Hardwicke had views of the Gothic Tower and the Prospect House engraved to circulate among his friends, with accompanying verses, and there was great excitement when Wimpole views, including these two garden buildings, were included in the designs of the Imperial Russian dinner service which Wedgwood made in 1774 for Catherine the Great.

The walls of Wimpole were gradually filling with portraits of the Yorke family and their spouses and children. The Earl had two daughters but no son; his heir was Philip, or 'Philly' as the family always called him, eldest son of his younger brother, the Hon. Charles Yorke, who had died in January 1770 in an agony of indecision about whether to accept the office of Lord Chancellor when it finally came to him in the Duke of Grafton's administration. The Earl of Hardwicke took a keen interest thereafter in the education and welfare of his nephew, encouraging him to go on the Grand Tour – an opportunity which no previous member of the family had enjoyed – and was pleased about Philly's surprise engagement in 1782 to Elizabeth Lindsay.

When the newly married couple made their first joint visit to Wimpole in September 1782, they saw a house and estate on which work was largely complete; they began to undertake great works on their own Hertfordshire home, Hamels, from which they could watch the gradual decline of the 2nd Earl into illness and hypochondria. Finally, Lord Hardwicke died at his St James's Square house on 16 May 1790; his body was brought back to Wimpole to lie in the Chicheley Chapel beside his father's.

NOTES

1 P. C. Yorke (ed.), *The life and correspondence of Philip Yorke, Earl of Hardwicke* (1910), ii, p.558.

2 BL, Add MS 5823, fo. 135.

3 BL, Add MS 35351, fos 136v, 134v, 138v.

4 Wimpole MS, fo. 2.

5 BL, Add MS 5823, fo. 136.

6 BL, Add MS 5823, fo. 135.

7 Bodleian Library, MS Top.gen.d.14, fos 47–8.

8 Bedfordshire Record Office [Beds RO], L39/9a/6, p.117.

9 BL, Add MS 35679, fos 67–83.

10 BL, Add MS 35679, fo. 24.

11 Joyce Godber, *The Marchioness Grey of Wrest Park*, Bedfordshire Historical Record Society, xlvii (1968), p.53; Beds RO, L30/9a/6, p.117.

12 Beds RO, 9a/8, p.69; BL, Add MS 35351, fo. 429r.

13 BL, Add MS 36229, fos 150–4; Yorke (ed.), *Life and correspondence*, iii, p.486.

14 Quoted in David Watkin, *Athenian Stuart* (1982), p.55.

15 HMC, *Portland MSS*, vi, 29 November 1734.

16 Elizabeth Biddulph, *Charles Philip Yorke, 4th Earl of Hardwicke . . . a memoir* (1910), p.163; Peter Orlando Hutchinson (ed.), *The Diary and letters of His Excellency Thomas Hutchinson Esq* (Boston, 1886), ii, p.590.

17 Beds RO, 9a/9, p.125.

CHAPTER FOUR

THE 3RD AND 4TH EARLS OF HARDWICKE (1790–1873)

On 31 January 1779 Philip Yorke, presumptive heir to the earldom of Hardwicke, wrote from Naples on his tour of Italian antiquities to his uncle, the 2nd Earl. He described going to see Pompeii, Vesuvius and Paestum. 'The three temples of Paestum of the old Doric order', he wrote 'are magnificent buildings and I was astonished to find how perfect they are. An English architect by name Soane who is an ingenious young man now studying at Rome accompanied us thither and measured the buildings.'[1]

It was an auspicious meeting, for John Soane and his highly individual brand of Neo-classicism were to have one of the greatest architectural influences on Wimpole. At the time, Soane was a young and little-known architect, and most of his plans, like his work on Ickworth, had come to little. He was to soar to fame, with many country-house commissions, buildings like the Bank of England and the Dulwich Picture Gallery, a knighthood, and his own house and personal museum in Lincoln's Inn Fields (which remains much in the condition he left it when he died in 1837). That was all in the future when the young men met. Yorke was an above-average connoisseur, as his views on Paestum showed Soane, and the architect enjoyed the nobleman's patronage through the next two decades. In the early 1780s Soane designed alterations to Yorke's Hertfordshire house, Hamels, of which the lodge gates are the only survivors. A scheme for semi-detached cottages stayed on the drawing-board, but a dairy and a hot-house were built.

Then, very shortly after Yorke inherited the earldom, Soane was summoned to Wimpole. Great plans to transform the house and the estate were afoot. Soane and his assistant Guibert surveyed the house on 10 June 1790, measured drawings were produced, and within a fortnight Soane was on his way to discuss plans with his client.

The works, speedily accomplished within a very few years, fall into a number of categories. Most memorably, there were dramatic alterations to the interior of the house; there was a new farm; there were building works in the grounds; and finally a range of improvements across the estate.

Of all these works, the most striking is the Yellow Drawing Room, one of Soane's most bravura country-house interiors. By knocking various ground- and first-floor rooms together, adding strengthening arches in the basement and half-filling Chicheley's still-surviving east back court with a new service staircase, Soane inserted a huge room into the house, keyhole-shaped in plan, L-shaped in section. ('Inserted' is appropriate: attic bedrooms were destroyed to accommodate the barrel vault, and the remnants of their windows, walls and fireplaces still hang suspended above it.) The inner part of the drawing-room comprises a circular top-lit space which rises through the full height of the house to a dome, with semi-circular apses on either side, while the outer contains a barrel-vaulted space lit by great windows looking north into the landscape. By knocking this room into the structure:

every purpose of convenience and magnificence is attained without disturbing any of the material parts of the building and further might be completed without incommoding the family.[2]

Such were the practicalities. There were also aesthetic reasons and classical associations. Soane's designs for the wall treatments, of yellow silk panels with dark borders decorated with arabesques, were reminiscent of the sort of decoration that was being unearthed in Rome when Soane and Yorke were both there. The domed end of the room has a sense of one of the great side chapels in the basilica of St John Lateran, which Soane had sketched. He sub-

View of the Drawing Room at Wimpole

The Earl of Hardwicke

Soane's proposal drawing for the Yellow Drawing Room
(Sir John Soane's Museum)

sequently presented a large copy of his drawing to Yorke who gave the picture a prominent place in Wimpole. Above all, the Yellow Drawing Room recalls the loggia of the Villa Madama, the mid-sixteenth-century villa in Rome built by Raphael, for which a series of Soane's measured drawings is preserved in his Museum. The villa also had a central domed space with lateral apses and a barrel-vaulted section leading to the gardens, an appropriate precedent for this pleasure room at Wimpole. The classical garden theme was carried through into the marble chimney-piece Soane installed at the south end of the Drawing Room, 'enriched with mouldings and carving consisting of Vitruvian scroll and foliage of husks, flowers, honeysuckles and four antique Grecian flowers in blockings'.[3]

Another characteristically Soanian scheme of decoration, including the chimney-piece with black marble panels and ormolu fittings, and black urns set in semi-circular niches, was used on his extension to Gibbs's Book Room, connecting through by double doors to the greenhouse, to accommodate more of the Hardwicke library. At the other end of the house a small service courtyard to the north of the Chapel was filled in to house a new plunge bath.

The idea of the plunge bath was by this time rather old-fashioned. Systems for bathing, equipped with hot and cold water, had been installed in the Palace of Whitehall in the 1670s and at Chatsworth in the 1690s, while Blenheim and Canons followed suit in the early eighteenth century. Such baths were usually used for reasons of health rather than cleanliness. Dr Oliver's *Practical Dissertation on the Bath Waters* of 1707 recommended dips in cold water, preferably mineral springs, as a remedy for headaches, impotence, the vapours and a variety of other maladies. Those who actually visited spas like Bath, and took their health seriously, often wished to continue the treatment when they returned home, so that in the mid-eighteenth century bath houses became quite common appendages to the English country house. Usually they were placed in the park some way away from the house to make the object of an outing, since they were used on a weekly or even monthly rather than a daily basis. Examples designed by Capability Brown still exist at Corsham and Burghley. That at Wimpole is a

rare instance of an indoor bath with heated water formed on the same principle which has survived the improvements of later Victorian and Edwardian 'sanitation'.

Soane's bath ingeniously remedied what had been hitherto lacking at Wimpole, and his addition, like the Yellow Drawing Room, was a daring way of successfully filling an awkward space. To provide water for the bath and the reorganised kitchen block beyond it, Soane made considerable improvements in a new water system fed from the *Castello d'Aqua* which he built in the grounds to replace the old reservoir and well head. The domed *Castello d'Aqua*, with its triumphal steps and urns in the niches on the three corners, has not survived.

The great window on the main staircase (where Burnet's portrait now hangs) was blocked up to

Soane installed the characteristically ornate chimney-piece in the Book Room

accommodate the new service staircase and a great skylight introduced to illuminate the stairs. On the first floor, Soane reorganised the rooms which ran through the centre of the house, providing a top-lit lobby with rooms leading off idiosyncratically shaped dressing-rooms in place of the upper gallery, and a grand semi-circular drawing-room (not open to the public). A new sense of dramatic space filled the house interiors, and the general redecoration of the rooms blew away the cobwebs of the first two earls' formal and rather old-fashioned living arrangements.

Soane's greatest contribution to the estate at Wimpole survives more or less intact: the home farm. Many great estates were vying with each other in the later eighteenth century in improving their farm buildings and agricultural techniques. Such 'improvement' was the fashionable excitement, and architects indulged landowners' flights of fancy just as much as landowners indulged the architects. Lady Grey had been almost apologetic that she and the 2nd Earl of Hardwicke had not gone in for agricultural improvement, the enclosure of land or new crop rotations, either at Wrest or at Wimpole.[4] Their nephew repaired those omissions.

The centrepiece of his enterprise was the farm that Soane designed.

In the farm buildings and in the labourers' cottages that Soane built for Wimpole, two strands of late eighteenth-century aesthetics combine. On the one hand, there was the practicality of farm improvement and the coaxing of the labourer to work more effectively. On the other hand, Lord and Lady Hardwicke were able to contemplate the antique and the pastoral, just as they could from the Yellow Drawing Room. At Hamels, Soane had designed and built a dairy for Elizabeth Yorke in 1781, with a separate room for taking tea, 'the strawberry room', with cream of course. (Soane's accounts show that he even provided romantic novels for Mrs Yorke to read there.) The dairy was an architectural essay based on the idea of the primitive hut, the columns being 'the trunks of elm trees with the bark on, and honeysuckles and woodbines planted at their feet forming festoons.' Such ideas were taken a stage further at Wimpole: in the summer of 1794 Soane drew up schemes for a dairy and a model home farm built around a yard, dominated by a great barn that filled most of one side. The design was one of many that Soane had

The 'Castello d'Aqua', built by Soane in the grounds to supply water to the house. It was demolished in the nineteenth century

(Opposite page) The 3rd Earl of Hardwicke, by George Romney (Yellow Drawing Room)

developed in the previous ten or fifteen years, and the Hardwickes gave his ideas free rein.

The farm buildings are an exercise in wood and thatch, a practical interpretation of the vernacular and an essay on the rustic sublime. Soane included a farmhouse and a dairy in his designs, but in the event neither was built. The dairy was to have been a more elaborate, octagonal version of that built at Hamels; alternative designs exist for it, each more bizarre than the last. The dairy had been sited by William Emes, the garden designer called in by Lord Hardwicke in 1790 to effect the final land-scaping of the park, 'the front to be in the wood' with a poultry yard behind it, so underlining the rustic character of the designs.[5]

Work on the farm occupied the labourers and craftsmen from May 1794, when the foundations were dug, to January 1795 when the barn and cowsheds were thatched. Meanwhile, building activity continued elsewhere on the estate. A new set of lodge gates was built from the main road at Arrington, extensive rebuilding took place at the Arrington Inn (to be renamed the Hardwicke Arms), a larger and more efficient hot-house was installed in the walled garden, and a number of cottages were built, most in brick – but one in mud, or *pisé* (a material then fashionable for self-con-sciously rustic vernacular buildings). After the mid-1790s Soane did little more work at Wimpole, although he still did occasional jobs at the Hard-wickes' house in St James's Square, as well as schemes for their relations. In 1819 he drew up a variety of plans for opening the Chicheley chapel to the parish church by inserting arches in the dividing wall, but these were not proceeded with. Mean-while, the Arrington lodges were subsiding and cracking, a problem which exercised Soane's office (and would eventually lead to their demolition).[6]

Lord Hardwicke aimed to be a model estate owner and employer: he instituted prizes for the best-kept cottage gardens, and was a leading ad-vocate of agricultural change. Lady Hardwicke founded a Sunday School (a design for one was among the first estate drawings Soane undertook), and would not allow a beerhouse on the estate. Political preferment took the couple away from Wimpole and England in the six years from 1801,

when Lord Hardwicke was appointed the first post-Union Viceroy of Ireland. He acquitted himself well in what was undoubtedly a difficult appoint-ment. A sequence of armed insurrections made the English nervous, especially during the Napoleonic wars, when Ireland was a potential staging post for an invader. Hardwicke was also supposed to main-tain an anti-Catholic policy with which he was fundamentally out of sympathy. Yet he successfully steered a middle course: 'Merely by a temperate exercise of the existing laws,' an observer wrote, Hardwicke 'has more advanced the strength of government, and its credit, than could be well conceived.'[7] He was rewarded with the Order of the Garter, and in spring 1806 returned to London and thence to Wimpole.

The 3rd Earl had continued, despite the pressures of his office, to maintain an interest in what was happening back in Cambridgeshire. In 1801 the latest star in the gardening world, Humphry Rep-ton, had been commissioned to work at Wimpole. In one of his famous Red Books, which he used to show his clients what wonders he hoped to perform, using 'before and after' illustrations, Repton made a series of recommendations. Denigrating the work of his predecessors, especially 'the bald system of modern gardening which has been so justly ridi-culed in the attacks on Mr Brown and his followers', Repton advocated a series of carriage drives through the woods on the eastern side, and reinstatement of the garden immediately around the house. 'I am aware of the prejudices which prevail in modern gardening against everything that seems to partake of artificial management', he wrote, adding that:

there is no part of Mr Brown's system which I have had more difficulty in correcting than the absurd fashion of bringing cattle to the windows of a house. It is called natural, but to me it has ever appeared unnatural that a palace should rise immediately out of a sheep pasture, or rather that one side of a house should not have a clear and protected communication with the pleasure grounds and flower gardens . . .

Here Repton's advice was taken some years later, and a north garden was enclosed with piers and railings, essentially that which survives today. 'Athenian' Stuart's Prospect House had by this time fallen into sad decline: when the Rev. James

Humphry Repton's 1801 Red Book for Wimpole proposed colour washing the exterior of the house, but his plans were not adopted

Plumptre saw it in July 1800, he was saddened by the state of 'one of the most elegant buildings I ever remember . . . The pillars which supported the centre were rotting away and the building supported by rough props . . . the pavement and steps torn up, and the place made a shelter for deer and sheep . . .'[8] Repton advised making the upper storey into a prospect room with the lower floor converted into a labourer's cottage (a change which seems to have been carried out). He also recommended that the other park building, the Gothic Tower on Johnson's Hill, would be made more useful by converting it into a keeper's lodge, and indeed a gamekeeper was still living there in the 1940s.

Various other Repton proposals, like colour-washing the whole of the big house, turning the row of eighteenth-century plain brick cottages into a rose-covered arbour, and even sailing a boat on the lake to signify the presence of water in the view from the house, were not taken up. This was the last major scheme to be commissioned for Wimpole's grounds; estate improvement continued on the farms, and Lord Hardwicke's agricultural interests were rewarded by his holding briefly the Presidency of the Board of Agriculture in 1814. William Cobbett described the Earl as 'a gentleman chiefly distinguished for his good library in St James's Square, and understanding the fattening of sheep as well as any man in Cambridgeshire.'[9]

Family interests became dominant. The Hardwickes had four daughters but no male heirs to survive them: their eldest son Philip, Lord Royston was drowned on his return from the Grand Tour in April 1808, and their surviving younger son died of scarlet fever two years later. After Lord Royston died, 'the most precious object at Wimpole . . . was the exquisite portrait of "Philip Yorke with a dog" which had been painted in his infancy by Sir Joshua Reynolds.'[10] (The portrait is now at Kenwood, in London.) However, family life continued with its mixture of fun and high-minded seriousness. Lady Hardwicke wrote a series of plays that she and the family performed in the Gallery at Wimpole, turning it into an impromptu theatre by hanging curtains across one of the screens of columns. One of her plays, *The Court of Oberon, or the Three Wishes*, was to be republished a number of times, and reissued in 1831 'in aid of the distressed Irish'. Her daughter, Lady Elizabeth Stuart, wrote to her in 1820, 'Now pray don't get too keen about cowhouses or hen-houses, and stand in the cold planning improvements', which suggests that old habits died hard.[11]

In 1834 the 3rd Earl died, and Westmacott was later commissioned to sculpt a life-size recumbent effigy of him in his Garter robes for the Chicheley chapel. He was succeeded by his nephew Charles Philip Yorke, son of the 3rd Earl's half-brother, Vice-Admiral Sir Joseph Yorke and himself a seafaring man for the previous sixteen years. (Four intervening heirs had predeceased the 3rd Earl before Charles Philip Yorke could inherit.) The new 4th Earl ruled over Wimpole for nearly forty years, the great Victorian *paterfamilias*, known on account of his naval background as 'Old Blowhard',

The 4th Earl of Hardwicke

'a martinet of the old school on his own quarter-deck'. One frequent visitor recalled, more charitably, 'He always brought a picture of the sea before me, his fine healthy colour, his brilliant dark eyes with their quick glance, his language, racy, to the point, original, direct – all seeming to belong to the old seafaring world.'[12]

Yorkes filled the place. The 4th Earl had four sons and three daughters, and his brother, the Venerable Henry Yorke, who held the living of Wimpole and occupied the Rectory, had another six children. (Some of them are depicted in the paintings of cherubs at play added in the lunettes of the Yellow Drawing Room in 1845.) Theatrical traditions using the Gallery continued within the family, under the direction of another of the 4th Earl's brothers, the Hon. Eliot Yorke, MP for Cambridgeshire.

From 1834 when he succeeded his uncle until his death, Lord Hardwicke held the Lord-Lieutenancy of Cambridgeshire, and he and his brother fought valiantly for the agricultural interest of the county. Sir Robert Peel had recommended Lord Hardwicke for the honour, and when Peel returned to office in 1841 the Earl was appointed Lord-in-Waiting to the Queen. A succession of royal engagements ensued. He accompanied the King of Prussia on his visit in 1842, striking up a friendship which resulted in Lord Hardwicke being invited there the following year, and entertaining Tsar Nicholas I on his visit to England in 1844. Meanwhile, Queen Victoria and Prince Albert had visited Wimpole for two days in October 1843, an event which was to be talked about for years after.

The event was that mixture of formality and contained chaos which often seems to mark royal visits. 'Our evening yesterday was formal', the Queen's Maid of Honour wrote on 26 October about the reception in the Yellow Drawing Room:

Lady Williamson could not come, so there was no music for Lady Hardwicke said she would not sing without her; consequently we sat or stood, and the Queen made her little civil speeches to everybody . . . [The next morning] you may imagine what a general rush there was, and how horrified poor Lady Hardwicke felt, to think that the Queen should have walked in [to the Chapel for morning prayers] and found nothing but the servants; however, it should not signify; she was very gracious, and only laughed . . .[13]

In the 1840s Kendall built this elaborate turreted conservatory (since demolished) to replace the existing orangery on the west end of the house; watercolour possibly by Thomas Allom

The coming royal visit and his position at court persuaded Lord Hardwicke that his house was not sufficiently large for the entertainment of such eminent personages as he had hopes of receiving. Although general redecoration and repairs had been undertaken around 1830, Wimpole again needed attention. The architect Henry Edward Kendall, who had had a prolific career which benefited from his facility of turning his hand to whichever style was chosen, designed considerable extensions and modifications to the house in 1842. On the main frontage, he added a large entrance porch, placed a statuary group representing Charity over the central pediment, added a balustrade to the roofline, and remodelled the chimneys. Huge new wings with towers at each end were added on the sides, extending an already long building into one some 400 feet in length. On the west, the orangery (last internally modified by Repton) was replaced by a turreted conservatory, while on the east a huge symmetrical kitchen and service block was built. Inside the house, many plaster ceilings were created or embellished, often in a conscious pastiche of the early eighteenth-century work. Within ten years, in a new building phase, Kendall had replaced Soane's near-derelict Arrington entrance lodges with a grand gateway, and replaced the stables to the south-west of the house with his own neo-baroque confection in striking red brick.

Kendall's work was the last major change to the fabric of Wimpole (but much of what he did has since been demolished). He gave the 4th Earl – at a cost of £100,000 – a house of which he felt proud, and to which the Prince of Wales would be a frequent visitor. New plantations and carriage drives added to the scenic interest of the park. On the political front, Lord Hardwicke – who had broken with Peel in 1846 over the repeal of the Corn Laws – returned to office with Lord Derby's ministry in 1852, when he was Postmaster-General for nine months, and then became Lord Privy Seal in 1858–9.

The 4th Earl 'was a good agriculturist, identifying himself with all the interests of the land, and resolutely opposing any changes which he considered detrimental to the interest of the country.'[14] He took an active personal interest in the running of the estate, hiring estate workers himself, providing schools and cottages, and overseeing his steward's accounts. Reading between the lines of his daughter's memoir of him, he was a hard taskmaster: 'He settled things in his own way, sometimes differing from ordinary routine,' she recalled, 'but he was scrupulously just, liberal and kind, with a most attractive sense of humour.'[15] Meanwhile, his connections saw that most of his children were given positions at court and married into the higher ranks of society. Soon after his son Eliot, equerry to the Duke of Edinburgh, was married at Wimpole in 1873 to Annie de Rothschild, Lord Hardwicke left for London and then his house, Sydney Lodge, on Southampton Water. There he died on 17 September, possessed of estates of 19,000 acres in Cambridgeshire and a few small properties besides. It was the beginning of the end of the Hardwickes at Wimpole.

NOTES

1 BL, Add MS 35378, fo. 305v.

2 Soane Museum, Drawer 6, set 1, no. 6.

3 Soane Museum, Drawer 45, set 2, nos 16–19; MS *Wimpole Account book [B]*, entries 17 May 1792.

4 Joyce Godber, *The Marchioness Grey of Wrest Park*, Bedfordshire Historical Record Society, xlvii (1968), pp.93–4.

5 Soane Museum, Drawer 64, set 6, esp. nos 22–26, 42, 46; fo. IV, nos 172–4.

6 Soane Museum, Drawer 47, set 1; Correspondence, XIII, G, *passim*.

7 G.E.C., *Complete peerage*, iii, p.307.

8 Cambridge University Library, Add MS 5819, transcribed by Ian Ousby.

9 G.E.C., *Complete peerage*, iii, p.307.

10 Augustus J. C. Hare, *The story of two noble lives* (1893), i, p.22.

11 Hare, *Two nobles lives*, i, p.112.

12 David Ellison (ed.), Alexander Campbell Yorke, *Wimpole as I knew it* (Bassingbourn, n.d.), p.17; G.E.C., *Complete peerage*, iii, p.307.

13 Mrs Stuart Erskine (ed.), *Twenty years at court: from the correspondence of Hon. Eleanor Stanley* (1916), pp.63–4.

14 Elizabeth P. Biddulph, *Charles Philip Yorke, 4th Earl of Hardwicke . . . a memoir* (1910), p.166.

15 Biddulph, *Charles Philip Yorke*, p.298.

CHAPTER FIVE

WIMPOLE SINCE 1873

Whereas the 4th Earl, despite considerable expenditure on the estate, left Wimpole in a strong financial position, his son and heir rapidly ran his inheritance into the ground. Known variously as 'Champagne Charlie' and 'the Glossy Peer', the 5th Earl of Hardwicke was a conspicuous adornment of the circle around the Prince of Wales (who as an undergraduate stayed frequently at Wimpole) and of the racecourse. After service in the Army in India he held the Cambridgeshire parliamentary seat for the Conservatives for eight years until gaining his inheritance; meanwhile he held office at court, as Comptroller of the Royal Household between 1866

The 5th Earl of Hardwicke, whose extravagance forced the sale of Wimpole to the 2nd Lord Robartes

and 1868 and then as Master of the Buckhounds until 1880. His lack of success in racing became legendary, as he steadily worked his way through the family fortune. 'I can see him now,' Lady Battersea wrote,

in faultless attire, with his carefully arranged satin tie, his beautiful pearl pin, his lustrous hat balanced at a certain angle on his well brushed hair, his coat sleeves always showing precisely the same amount of white cuff, his pleased-with-himself-and-the-world expression.

His portrait photographs show just that smug look. Within fifteen years of inheriting Wimpole, he had amassed debts of almost £300,000, mainly with the Agar-Robartes Bank; and Wimpole, which he only rarely graced with his presence, and that usually during the shooting season, had to go.

Although there was considerable interest in the sale, which took place in August 1891, Wimpole failed to reach its reserve price. Three years later, in satisfaction of the 5th Earl's huge debts, the 2nd Lord Robartes took over the house and estate in his capacity as Chairman of Agar-Robartes Bank. After two hundred years, the Wimpole estate and Lanhydrock, in Cornwall, were both reunited in the hands of the Robartes, who were directly descended from the 2nd Earl of Radnor; and both houses have since passed into the care of the National Trust.

Lord Hardwicke's eldest son, 'left in the House of Lords without a shilling' as he put it, joined a City firm of stockbrokers. Champagne Charlie left Wimpole for the last time in 1894, and died three years later. The entail on the estate had had to be broken, with the permission of his son and brother, the next in line to inherit, to save the 5th Earl from the ignominy of being declared bankrupt. The Robartes family agreed to pay annuities to the 5th Earl and his two daughters for life, as a final charge on the estate.

Lord Robartes may have had ancestral connections with Wimpole, but he enjoyed it as his
principal country residence only briefly, since in
1897 he succeeded his cousin to become 6th Viscount Clifden and so moved to Lanhydrock, the
Clifdens' main seat. Lord Clifden served, as owners
of Wimpole frequently had, as Lord-Lieutenant of
Cambridgeshire for a number of years, and Wimpole continued to be used for shooting parties, social
gatherings and family holidays. Lord Clifden was
passionately fond of cricket, and memories are still
fresh for some local people of the cricket matches in
front of the house, especially the day in 1922 when
all 22 members of two visiting police cricket teams
plunged into Soane's bath to cool off. Often
Wimpole was shut up, a great ghost from the past.
Lord Clifden settled Wimpole on his son Gerald in
1906 when he joined the Diplomatic Service,

apparently with the words 'You must have a place
of your own, my boy – you'll find they all do.'
When the 6th Viscount died in 1930, the mainten-
ance of both Lanhydrock and Wimpole proved to
be an expensive nightmare, and Gerald Agar-
Robartes, as 7th Viscount Clifden, felt obliged to
move to Lanhydrock. The contents of Wimpole
had been gradually stripped, finding their way to
Lanhydrock or the sale rooms; the house was let to
tenants, the last of whom were Captain and Mrs
George Bambridge in 1936, at a quarterly rent of
£225.

It is with the Bambridges that the sad decline of
Wimpole was brought to an end. Elsie Bambridge
was the only surviving child of Rudyard Kipling,
who died soon after she moved into Wimpole. As
his heiress, she was able to use the substantial royalties from his books to buy and then to refurbish the

*The Agar-Robartes
family, c.1910:
(from left to right)
Lady Clifden, her
daughter Everilda, and
Lord Clifden*

house over the next forty years. Kipling, on his only visit to the house, is supposed to have warned her: 'Bird, I hope you have not bitten off more than you can chew!' Loving the house, she made preserving Wimpole her life's work.

George Bambridge had been at prep school and at Eton with Gerald Agar-Robartes, and had shot at Wimpole on a number of occasions in his youth. The son of the former secretary to the Duke of Edinburgh (to whom the Hon. Eliot Yorke had been equerry), he was born in 1892. With the outbreak of the First World War, he joined the Middlesex Regiment and later transferred to the Irish Guards. In April 1918 he was wounded in the battle for Arras and subsequently was awarded the Military Cross. 'It was entirely due to his initiative and dash', the *London Gazette* citation read, 'that the line was maintained.' It was probably in the war that Bambridge had first made contact with the Kiplings, for John Kipling, Rudyard's only son, was also in the Irish Guards. John was killed in action in 1916, which proved a savage blow to the family. After 1920 Bambridge entered the Diplomatic Service, and in 1924 he married Elsie Kipling. For more than ten years he led a diplomat's life, as Honorary Attaché at the British Embassies in Madrid, Brussels and finally Paris. The Bambridges were generous entertainers, and, when George Bambridge left the Service in 1933, they returned to England looking for a new home.

For a few years they lived in Burgh House, Hampstead, but they really wanted a country house. The Bambridges had considered taking a lease on Attingham Park in Shropshire, a house they had visited on one of their visits home in 1927, 'travelling through England in great pomp in an enormous motor full of luggage, with chauffeur and a Spanish valet in gorgeous footman's livery and yellow waistcoat!' Instead they took Wimpole on a lease, and in 1938 purchased it from Lord Clifden. Few of the furnishings remained, and fewer pictures (the portrait of Bishop Burnet being the major exception). The Bambridges had to start to fill their massive house from scratch.

The present contents of Wimpole, therefore, are largely the result of Captain and Mrs Bambridge's collecting on their travels and in the salerooms.

Captain and Mrs Bambridge in Paris in the early 1930s

Many items in the house, both pictures and furniture, are souvenirs of their years abroad – Spanish drawings of bullfighters, paintings of cityscapes, Paris porcelain. The immense numbers of sporting pictures and prints of carriages reflect the tastes and interests of Captain Bambridge. (His collection is described in more detail in Chapter Seven.)

During the 1930s, the Bambridges often entertained quite lavishly, their dining-room graced by footmen in powdered wigs and breeches for the grandest dinner parties. With wartime, Wimpole was largely put into mothballs, and the household moved into the basement, dining in the Servants' Hall, with the Bambridges themselves usually living in the old Housekeeper's Room beneath the Ante-Chapel. Wimpole was not blessed with many of the amenities that were becoming common even in old houses: the drainage and water supply remained primitive and there was no mains electricity. One frequent visitor at the time remembers 'those scarce flickering lights which progressively dimmed as the load on the ancient batteries increased. Oddly enough, the servants' quarters were fully electrified while the rest of the house was not, although neither had [mains] power.'

The house was not requisitioned by the War Office, put off both by lack of services and by pleas

An eighteenth-century pin print, one of the many objects collected by Captain and Mrs Bambridge to furnish Wimpole

from those, like the Professor of Botany at Cambridge, who did not want the precious park landscape destroyed. Instead, part of the estate on the Arrington side was taken over as an American army hospital. In 1943 George Bambridge died, as a result of a severe chill caught while out shooting; and his widow spent the next thirty years putting Wimpole to rights.

Our knowledge of Wimpole in these years is still very limited, since Elsie Bambridge became ever more reclusive. Those who worked for her had immense respect for their employer (one cook who came for two weeks to help out stayed fifteen years), but she placed little value on the opinions of people outside. Mrs Bambridge had very few visitors, and Wimpole was rarely opened to those interested in historic houses or their libraries. The American base, which became first a teacher-training college and then a home for squatters, was a constant source of irritation until its final demolition; and stories abound of Mrs Bambridge's irate reaction to anyone who tried to approach the house or strayed from footpath rights of way. Her fierce pride in Wimpole and its history was famous – when Sir

Nikolaus Pevsner visited on his researches for the Cambridgeshire volume of the *Buildings of England*, she was apparently annoyed because she had never before been contradicted so many times in the space of ten minutes. Other anecdotes suggest she did have a sense of humour: many versions circulate of the story – which is probably apocryphal, alas – of Elsie Bambridge spotting a couple picnicking beside their car in the grounds, taking down their car registration number, and turning up the following Sunday in her chauffeur-driven car, to have her lunch on the miscreants' front lawn.

In her latter years, Mrs Bambridge slid gently into senility, often believing she was in South Africa, or that visitors had arrived by boat. At her death in 1976 she bequeathed the house and the estate to the National Trust, except for a few legacies to servants, friends and relatives. She also instructed her executors to burn her diaries as well as those of her husband and her mother, which left even fewer clues to posterity of the Bambridge years. Wimpole, Cambridgeshire's grandest house, was an exciting bequest to the National Trust, with its many family associations, and the roll-call of celebrated architects and landscape designers who have worked there.

Creative adaptation is the key to Wimpole's history, each generation building on the achievements of its predecessor. Fifteen years of National Trust ownership have seen no change in that pattern. There have been major programmes of restoration on the house and the stables. The Home Farm buildings were rescued and restored as a centre for rare animal breeds (see Chapter Ten). The Gothic Tower, the western lake, the rotting Chinese bridge, have all been rescued and cleaned, and opened up to visitors by a network of waymarked paths and walks through the park. In some ways most exciting, although least visible, a thorough investigation of the park and gardens has revealed how many vestiges of previous occupiers from the Romans and the medieval manorial tenants to the Victorian Hardwickes and the Bambridges have survived. The layers of time have been peeled back at Wimpole Hall, revealing the contribution which each generation from Chicheley to Bambridge has made.

CHAPTER SIX

THE BOOKS

Whether Thomas Chicheley, the builder of the 'curious neat house' at Wimpole, or his successor, Charles Robartes, collected books we do not know. By contrast we know almost too much about the collecting habits of Edward Harley. He is said at the time of his death in 1741 to have accumulated some 8,000 volumes of manuscripts, 50,000 printed books, perhaps 350,000 pamphlets, 41,000 prints and dozens of albums of drawings. The character of the Harleian collection and the transformation of Wimpole to accommodate it are described in Chapter Two. The only surviving vestiges at Wimpole are a few prayer books in the Chapel, as Harley's extravagance, his subsequent bankruptcy, drinking and dissolution obliged his widow to sell the entire collection. In 1740, then, the next owner, Lord Chancellor Hardwicke was faced with many empty shelves at Wimpole. Fortunately for the look of the place his collection of books was by no means inconsiderable.

The allocation of particular volumes which still survive at Wimpole among the first three earls is not easy: irritatingly sharing the same Christian name, they more irritatingly used the same bookplate. However, before his advancement to the earldom in 1754, Baron Hardwicke of Hardwicke in the county of Gloucester proudly caused a bookplate bearing that style, addition and title to be affixed to many books. These books are also rather distinctive: the assumption seems fair that similar ones bearing the 'Philip Earl of Hardwicke' plate are likely to have been his too.

And how should one characterise Chancellor Hardwicke's books? As a collection it is rich in early – or rather, old-fashioned – literature. It contained, for example, a lot of sixteenth- and seventeenth-century vernacular literature, much in French and Italian; but a notable number of Spanish books are present too – this is not usual. There are, as well, English books of the same period, many of them associated with the sectarian controversies which raged as the Anglican church emerged, but were rather old hat in Hanoverian England. Was the Lord Chancellor of an antiquarian bent? It was not an uncommon weakness amongst lawyers. The answer is simple, if not obvious.

In 1716 Lord Chancellor Somers died. Hardwicke was married to his niece and the old man left the promising young lawyer half of his books. In 1729, therefore, after the expiry of a life interest, Hardwicke, then Attorney-General, shared his uncle's books with the Master of the Rolls, Sir Joseph Jekyll. Sadly, few specific books are listed in the record of the division made,[1] but the categories are interesting. So, too, are the values put upon these categories. Many are predictable: *Jus Anglicanum*, each received £62 8s worth; others not so: *Historia Polonica etc*, £2 10s; and *Poetae Hispanici*, a mere 9s 6d. The division also reveals Hardwicke's preference for particular subjects, notably geography and old bibles. Each got books worth £1,572 10s 2d.

The bookplate of Baron Hardwicke of Hardwicke, later created 1st Earl of Hardwicke

Philip Lord Hardwicke
Baron of Hardwicke
in ye County of Gloucester.

Somers was obviously a considerable collector; that he was a man of an earlier generation explains the somewhat old-fashioned tinge to the books at Wimpole.

The collection now is not as it was in Hardwicke's time. In 1792 the Lord Chancellor's grandson, the 3rd Earl, disposed of 'the duplicate part of the Library of a nobleman': a misnomer, as such books included in the sale as can now be identified were not duplicated in the house. The vendor's intention was not philistine, however; recently come into his

'The eruption of Vesuvius', an illustration from Sir William Hamilton's 'Campi Phelegraei' (1779) in the Wimpole Library

inheritance he was spending money to create the Book Room – perhaps the most beautiful room in the house. Less sympathy may perhaps be expended on the 5th Earl, 'Champagne Charlie', who sold 'An important portion of the valuable library, formed during the last century by Lord Chancellor Hardwicke' in 1888: Caxtons, Pynsons and Wynkyn de Wordes were amongst those offered. It is interesting that even 120 years after his death Hardwicke's name was considered a selling point. Many of the books sold were like those known to have come from Somers and may have been his. From the dates of publication, some must have been bought originally by the 2nd or 3rd Earls.

The Somers-Hardwicke books which remain at Wimpole by no means comprise the whole collection. Besides those added by the 2nd and 3rd Earls, the Lord Chancellor's younger son Charles added many classical texts in the excellent 'modern' editions of the eighteenth century. The collection was enchanced too by books from the library at Tittenhanger in Hertfordshire formed by Thomas Pope Blount, the grandfather of Charles Yorke's wife, books in sort and quality not unlike Somers's. As in most libraries, the precise provenance of many cannot be determined – who, for example, was responsible for the wonderful 14 volumes of Piranesi?

As we have seen, the 5th Earl trod a path not uncommon for the Victorian aristocrat. The Library at Wimpole was treated like many others: books were not for reading, they were for selling. The 2nd Lord Robartes subsequently reduced the collection still further, but the depredations he made were slight: a few dozen books were removed to Lanhydrock where they still remain. Mrs Bambridge on the other hand enhanced the collection by adding her own books and those of her husband; more important, perhaps, she also added books from the library of her mother and father, and some rare editions of Kipling are now at Wimpole. She added notably to what is still a notable collection: picked it may have been, but much of the historical heart remains.

44

CHAPTER SEVEN
THE PICTURES

The collection of pictures formed by Capt. and Mrs Bambridge is the third of any consequence to have been hung at Wimpole. The first was that of Edward, Lord Harley, 2nd Earl of Oxford. One of the greatest virtuosi of his – or any – day, he was an outstanding collector and patron of the visual arts, especially of Gibbs, Rysbrack, Dahl (see Chapter Two), Wootton, from whom he commissioned over forty pictures, Thornhill (see Chapter Eight), Zincke and Vertue. Unfortunately, the debts that he left forced his widow to disperse his collection of sculpture, some three hundred Old Master paintings (primarily Italian Baroque) and portraits of famous persons, in a six-day sale held in March 1742. 'All the family pictures of the Cavendishes, Holles', Pierponts, Harleys, etc., Noblemen, Ladys and gentlemen in any ways related, my lady reserved for her own use not to be sold.' These were taken to her daughter's seat, Welbeck Abbey in Nottinghamshire, where, as Horace Walpole wrote, she 'passed her whole widowhood, except in doing ten thousand right and just things, in collecting and monumenting [i.e. inscribing] the portraits and reliques of all the great families from which she descended, and which centred in her.' No doubt because they reflected her own love of hunting she also exempted from sale and took with her to Welbeck virtually all Wootton's horse and animal paintings, but not his landscapes. Eleven of these Woottons have kindly been lent back by her descendant, Lady Anne Cavendish-Bentinck.

The second collection was that of the Earls of Hardwicke. The cream of Lord Chancellor Hardwicke's Old Masters was hung in Flitcroft's Gallery, including works by Rubens, Teniers, Cuyp and Titian. The 2nd Earl of Hardwicke was both a collector of pictures and an active patron. Reynolds wrote of the failure of 'our scheme of ornamenting St Paul's with Pictures', and encouraged Lord Hardwicke to commission a picture of an interview between James II and the Duke of Monmouth. Gainsborough painted the Earl in 1763 (when he was still Lord Royston), and explained his attitude to landscape: 'with respect to *real Views* from Nature in this Country he has never seen any Place that affords a Subject equal to the poorest imitations of Gaspar or Claude . . . if his Lordship wishes to have anything tolerable of the name of G., the subject altogether, as well as figures &c., must be of his own Brain; otherwise Lord Hardwicke will only pay for Encouraging a Man out of his way, and had much better buy a picture of some of the good Old Masters.' Unfortunately, Gainsborough's strictures

'The Countess of Oxford's Dun Mare and Thomas Thornton the Groom', by John Wootton (Entrance Hall). Lord Oxford was Wootton's most important patron

seem to have discouraged the 2nd Earl from commissioning any landscape at all from him. Indeed, apart from Reynolds's portrait of his great-nephew, *Master Philip Yorke* (now at Kenwood), few of his important commissions appear to have remained long at Wimpole. The 2nd Earl's acquisition of Wright of Derby's *Earth-Stopper* (1773; Derby Art Gallery) showed his discrimination in buying unconventional pictures by contemporary artists, but also shed a less attractive light on his parsimony. Wright had gone to Italy by the time that Lord Hardwicke had agreed to buy it for 50 guineas (he might have expected double that sum), so he wrote back to the Secretary of the Society of Artists: 'The shabby price his Lordship is to pay for it will leave no room for his Lordship to expect the frame with it . . . on no account let him have it.'

Soane created the Yellow Drawing Room for the 3rd Earl to display the best of the Hardwicke collection, but curiously it does not seem to have been used for this purpose. When Gustav Waagen visited the house in 1854, the only picture that he mentioned in this room was the three-quarter length of the *3rd Earl of Hardwicke* by Lawrence (private collection), which the painter thought had 'consistent richness of effect'. Elsewhere, Flemish and Dutch pictures predominated, with a bias towards portraits of famous men, particularly lawyers, a number of which may have been survivals from Harley's collection. Two hundred of these pictures, including many of the 5th Earl of Hardwicke's own family portraits, were prepared for auction by Christie's in what must have been a hastily got-up sale to stave off financial disaster, on 7 August 1880. At the last minute, however, after the catalogue had been printed, the sale was called off; some of the pictures appear to have been bought privately by other members of the family, others to have been sold discreetly to dealers. A residue of 63 pictures was again sent to auction at Christie's, on 30 June 1888. None the less, a few non-family portraits remained at Wimpole: the magnificently framed Kneller of *Bishop Burnet in his Garter robes* (Great Staircase), also apparently the Richardson portrait of *George Vertue* (Gallery), then thought to be of Matthew Prior, and the Le Marchand ivory bust of *Lord Somers* (Library).

Wimpole never became the main seat of the Robarteses, Viscounts Clifden, so that even had the family not removed most of the contents to Lanhydrock when they sold the house, there would have been few pictures with which the Bambridges could have furnished it. As it was, they had no option but to install their own collection of pictures, accumulated during a life lived on a very different scale – at first in flats in the various European cities in which Capt. Bambridge had been serving and subsequently in Burgh House, Hampstead.

Capt. Bambridge always seems to have had the instincts of a collector, but he began with a compass both modest and narrow. His earliest interest seems to have been in prints, particularly of coaching scenes; despite – or even because of – his military background, he rarely seems to have collected military depictions, even when buying pictures by artists who specialised in that sort of subject, such as Alexander von Bensa or Max Claude. About 1926 he noted 'Constantin Guys 1840 (Look for his carriage books)', and the eleven drawings at Wimpole by or attributed to Guys testify that Guys remained an abiding passion. Later entries in the same notebook record print shops in Vienna, or the address of one in Dublin, annotated subsequently: 'Nothing much'; or the instruction to himself: 'Search shops in Rue de Seine, Paris', annotated subsequently: 'Done'. The very last entry is a select list of conversation-pieces shown at the pioneering 1930 exhibition of *English Conversation Pictures* mounted by Sir Philip Sassoon and Mrs David Gubbay, who bequeathed her fine collection of furniture and porcelain to the National Trust. It seems to have been this exhibition, and the books that followed on from it – G. C. Williamson's *English Conversation Pictures* (1931), to which Capt. Bambridge subscribed, and Sacheverell Sitwell's *Conversation Pieces* (1936) and *Narrative Pictures* (1937) – that gave a new turn to Capt. Bambridge's interests. In his foreword to *English Conversation Pictures*, Sir Philip Sassoon wrote, 'It is still more difficult to understand why, in these days of flats and smaller houses, [this form of painting] should not regain some measure at least of its old vogue.' This must have seemed sensible advice to the Bambridges, just back from leading a peripatetic existence in foreign capitals, and indeed, when they came to Wimpole, essentially they inhabited and installed their collections only in such rooms as could form a kind of flat within the shell of the huge house.

Very little documentary evidence for Capt. Bambridge's purchases has survived, but he does not seem to have begun collecting seriously until after he left the Diplomatic service in 1933. His previous life abroad made him particularly responsive to foreign pictures with an anecdotal interest. Sadly, Luis Paret's *Promenade in front of the Botanical Gardens in Madrid* eluded him, apparently because of the price. The first documented purchase, the anonymous *Figures promenading in front of a palace* (Ante Room) bought at Christie's in 1936 for 32 gns, is a pale substitute for this.

When Kipling died in 1936, his daughter was left in receipt of his royalties; it seems no coincidence that Capt. Bambridge's purchases started to quicken after this date, reaching a peak in 1940 and 1941, when prices were inevitably depressed by the war. In 1937 he bought the Hicks sketch and the two Tissots (Mrs Bambridge's Study); 1938 and 1939 seem to have been quiet – yet it is hard to think of

anyone else in England at that date who would have bought the Quinart of *The duc de Berry shooting an eagle* (Mrs Bambridge's Study). In 1940 he bought at least ten pictures. These included some English pictures, including two of the more eccentric examples from the sale of Arthur N. Gilbey's unique collection of angling pictures, and a Devis conversation-piece that had been a star of the 1930 exhibition (Ante Room). However, two were Yorke family portraits (Yellow Drawing Room) and one a large decorative flower-piece well-suited to fill a panel in the Saloon. These kinds of purchase were to be characteristic of Mrs Bambridge when she was left on her own – and indeed, may have been made at her suggestion.

Capt. Bambridge's purchases in 1941 included the most striking of all his foreign pictures – Thévenin's view of the complex of buildings erected for the cotton-magnate Richard-Lenoir by Charles Normand (Lord Chancellor's Dressing Room) – but also two of his most intriguing English pictures – Witherington's *Modern Picture Gallery* (Mrs Bambridge's Study) and the anonymous depiction of *Pattison's Shoe-Shop* (Lord Chancellor's Dressing Room). By 1942 the pace had slowed, no

'An angling party', by Edward Smith, 1773 (Ante Room). Bought by Captain Bambridge for Wimpole

doubt because the art market itself had now been paralysed by the war; but it is a characteristic sign of Capt. Bambridge's independence of mind that one of the two pictures that he is recorded as buying should have been German (Ante Room). His last purchase, *Master Graham* by Tilly Kettle in 1943 (South Drawing Room), demonstrates a taste for good or appealing portraiture for its own sake, which was also to be manifested by Mrs Bambridge.

From the testimony of all who knew her, Mrs Bambridge's prime motivation in later life was her love of Wimpole, and of anything that had associations with it or its owners. She bought mainly through Leggatt Bros., and then Oscar & Peter Johnson, but does not seem to have begun collecting in a vigorous way until the later 1950s, and only intermittently thereafter. It would appear that this coincided with a determination to tackle the emptiness of Wimpole, so that in these years she not only bought Chicheley and Yorke portraits, but also other big portraits and flower-pieces to fill the large spaces of the Saloon and Grand Staircase. Her last

'At the shoemaker's' (Lord Chancellor's Dressing Room). A rare view of a London shoe-shop in the 1820s

purchase appears to have been at the Hardwicke sale in 1967, the two Hudsons of *The Hon. Charles Yorke* and his wife *Catherine Freman* (Gallery).

Her enthusiasm for things with Wimpole associations had its blind spots, however, particularly over sculpture. She allowed Le Marchand's exceptional ivory bust of *Lord Somers*, which had stayed at Wimpole despite the death or removal of the Earl of Oxford and the Hardwickes and their sales, to elude her in 1939 (now happily restored to the house at the express wish of Mr Simon Houfe after the death of his grandfather and its eventual purchaser, Sir Albert Richardson). Mr Houfe also has an amusing account of an exchange between Sir Albert Richardson and Mrs Bambridge over some more sculpture that had been at Wimpole since Lord Harley's day, the busts of four Roman Emperors:

Mrs Bambridge had thrown out four of these because they were chipped, rather as one might dispose of an old Woolworth's tea-cup or a cracked jam-jar. These too arrived at Collins and Clarke's antique shop and found their way to Ampthill. When she discovered their destination she was slightly ruffled.
"I've got *your* Roman emperors," Grandfather laughingly announced to her one day.
Elsie Bambridge pealed with laughter.
"Those *terrible* old things!" she exclaimed.
"They are very fine and look magnificent on my loggia," he continued triumphantly.
This was too much for her and her eyes hardened into narrow slits.
"Terrible old things!" she insisted, "and very battered!"
"Not at all battered, dear lady," added my grandfather, ignoring the fact that three out of the four noses were repaired with dental cement, 'on the contrary, magnificent!'
"Battered!" protested Mrs Bambridge with eyes blazing and there the conversation ended![1]

These Emperors are still in Sir Albert Richardson's house, which is itself a work of art, so their loss from Wimpole is the more acceptable. None the less, the Trust continues to pursue Mrs Bambridge's aim of recovering works of art associated with Wimpole.

NOTES

1 Simon Houfe, *Sir Albert Richardson: The Professor* (London, 1980), p.157.

CHAPTER EIGHT

TOUR OF THE HOUSE

The Exterior

THE SOUTH FRONT AND FORECOURT

The extent of the seventeenth-century house built by Sir Thomas Chicheley is represented by the tall, central block of seven bays. It was refaced to a Palladianising design by Henry Flitcroft in 1742. The central element comprises a heavily rusticated porch, surmounted first by a Venetian window, and in turn by a Diocletian or 'therm' window; the pediment above bears the arms of the 1st Earl of Hardwicke when still a baron. The statue group representing Charity on the gable apex was carved by J. H. Foley, more celebrated for his statue of the Prince Consort at the centre of the Albert Memorial

in Hyde Park. The balustrading and the terracotta urns from M. H. Blanchard's manufactory are also Victorian.

The two balustraded wings of five bays to either side of the central block were added to the original house by James Gibbs between 1713 and 1721. The double-height space of the Chapel on the east side is expressed by blind sash windows at basement level. The façade, more than 250 feet long, was considerably longer prior to the removal in the 1950s of a conservatory to the west, and a service wing to the east, which had been built for the 4th Earl of Hardwicke by Henry Kendall in 1842. The stone urns and busts punctuating the forecourt screen were almost certainly designed by Gibbs for the once formal north gardens. Among the busts are allegories of Fortune, with a die and cornucopia, and Justice, with an eye-shaped pendant and scales,

The central block of the south front, refaced by Henry Flitcroft in 1742

PLANS OF THE HOUSE

Shaded areas
not open to the public

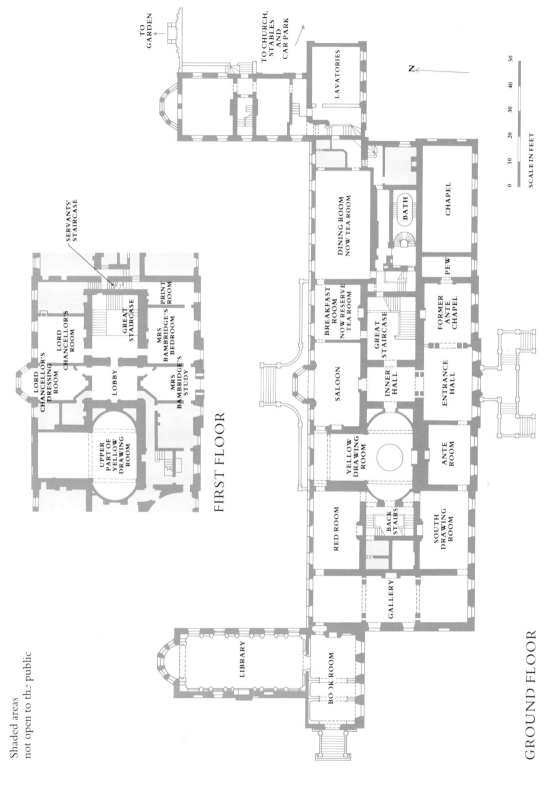

FIRST FLOOR

- LORD CHANCELLOR'S DRESSING ROOM
- LORD CHANCELLOR'S ROOM
- SERVANTS' STAIRCASE
- LOBBY
- GREAT STAIRCASE
- MRS BAMBRIDGE'S BEDROOM
- PRINT ROOM
- MRS BAMBRIDGE'S STUDY
- UPPER PART OF YELLOW DRAWING ROOM

GROUND FLOOR

- LIBRARY
- BOOK ROOM
- GALLERY
- RED ROOM
- BACK STAIRS
- YELLOW DRAWING ROOM
- SOUTH DRAWING ROOM
- ANTE ROOM
- SALOON
- INNER HALL
- ENTRANCE HALL
- BREAKFAST ROOM NOW RESERVE TEA ROOM
- GREAT STAIRCASE
- FORMER ANTE CHAPEL
- DINING ROOM NOW TEA ROOM
- BATH
- PEW
- CHAPEL
- LAVATORIES

TO GARDEN

TO CHURCH, STABLES AND CAR PARK

N

SCALE IN FEET
0 10 20 30 40 50

50

The north front

THE NORTH FRONT

The north façade of the Chicheley house was altered by Flitcroft in 1745. He heightened the attic storey and added a central two-storey oriel window with a therm window and pediment above. The pedimented surrounds of the six first-floor windows, the pair on the ground floor to either side of the central oriel, and the basement windows are probably survivals from the earlier façade. Not only are the first-floor windows set in large fields of roughly laid English bond brick typical of the seventeenth century, but there are traces on the stonework margins of mullion and transom stubs. It seems likely that Gibbs removed the then unfashionable stone mullions and inserted sashes; certainly, Flitcroft's 'Scheme of Works' of c.1744 specifies only the repair and cleaning of 'twelve Dresses to the old windows' of the Garden Front. Four of these, the large windows to the Yellow Drawing Room and Breakfast Room on the ground floor, were replaced by Soane, and are fitted with 'El-Dorado Sashes', patented by Keir & Co. in 1793. Kendall grouped the various chimneys in a massive central stack, which has been rebuilt by the Trust. The east wing seems only to have been a screen wall with mock windows until Kenton Couse formed his 'Eating Room' behind. The west Library wing was added by Gibbs in 1730, and the five-sided bay window inserted at the north end c.1754. Facing the Library is the laundry wing.

also Spring and Autumn. The largest vases correspond with a drawing by Gibbs in the Bodleian Library, and were carved by Andries Carpentière, Van Nost's protégé.

The Interior

The contents whenever possible are described CLOCKWISE FROM THE FAR END OF THE ROOM under their separate headings.

THE ENTRANCE HALL

Structurally part of Chicheley's original building, the Hall was slightly extended to the south in the course of Flitcroft's refacing work. It was subsequently made continuous with the Inner Hall by Sir John Soane, who replaced the dividing wall with a pair of Ionic columns *in antis* (carved by Edward Foxhall). This scheme may be seen in his perspective view from the Saloon (c.1791), now hanging in the Red Room. In the 1840s Kendall added a second pair of contrastingly ornate Ionic columns to the south of Soane's, and incorporated the former Ante-Chapel within the Entrance Hall by removing the wall dividing them and inserting a further pair of Ionic columns. Flitcroft's survey of 1742 shows a winding stair, now gone, in the north-east corner of the Ante-Chapel. The stair led down to the basements and Chapel proper, and was lit by a window facing on to the subsequently infilled east courtyard.

In 1735, according to a visiting antiquary, the Rev. Jeremiah Milles, the room was hung with religious pictures by Sir James Thornhill, and with portraits of Archbishop Laud and other Anglican divines by Michael Dahl. Soane remodelled the Ante-Chapel to create a curiously sited State Bedchamber, which had apsidal niches in the northern corners of the room. Hooks, which in the 1920s supported a row of leather fire-buckets, are still visible in the dentil course of the north wall ceiling architrave. The pew to the family chapel beyond the glazed door is set out with the few remnants of the Harleian library to survive at Wimpole. The bindings are original, and are emblazoned with the arms of Edward, Lord Harley (later 2nd Earl of Oxford), and his wife, Henrietta Cavendish-Holles, only daughter of the 1st Duke of Newcastle,

DECORATION

In 1948 Mrs Bambridge marbled the columns and pilasters green; they were returned to an earlier colour by the National Trust in the 1970s.

FIREPLACE

Eighteenth-century pink and white marble chimney-piece from Rosehaugh, Ross-shire, inserted by Mrs Bambridge. The separate, cast-iron fireback bears the Hardwicke initial and earl's coronet.

FLOOR

A highly decorative scheme of encaustic tiles from the Benthall Works of Maw & Co., Broseley, Shropshire, c.1880. The mosaic incorporates the Hardwicke monogram and motto NEC CUPIAS NEC METUAS – 'neither desire nor fear', while the threshold to the former Ante-Chapel bears the Latin greeting SALVE!

PICTURES

The majority of the paintings by John Wootton at Wimpole have kindly been lent back to the house by Lady Anne Cavendish-Bentinck. They are a representative fraction of the forty pictures commissioned from Wootton by Edward, Lord Harley, 2nd Earl of Oxford, who was not only Wootton's chief patron, but also introduced him to his circle of poets, artists and virtuosi.

(Clockwise, from the overmantel in the former Ante-Chapel; oil on canvas, unless otherwise stated.)

JOHN WOOTTON (c.1682–1764)
The Countess of Oxford's Dun Mare and Thomas Thornton the groom
Signed lower right: *J. Wootton.*
Although Wootton himself called this 'The Sketch of my Lady's Mare' in his bill of 1715, only the horse is the same as in his big painting of the subject (State Dining Room). It is in fact an independent picture, more sensitive in its portrayal of both groom and landscape. Henrietta, Countess of Oxford inherited the Newcastle family passion for horses: she was the only woman to be shown as the central figure in any

of Wootton's hunting scenes. The Dun Mare was doubtless one of her favourite mounts.

JOHN WOOTTON (c.1682–1764)
The Duke of Rutland's 'Bonny Black'
Signed on the scroll.
Wootton charged Edward, Lord Harley £12 18s in 1715. In 1711 he had painted a life-size portrait of the horse for its owner, which no doubt perished in the fire that devastated Belvoir Castle in Rutland in 1816.

Manner of JAN FRANS VAN BLOEMEN, called ORIZZONTE (1662–1749)
Pair of ideal landscapes
Bought by Mrs Bambridge in 1963.

JAN WEENIX (c.1642–1719)
Portrait of an Unknown Man
Signed on a letter at the left: *J. Weenix.*
Probably painted when Weenix was working in Düsseldorf for the Elector Palatine Jan Wellem between 1702 and 1716. The sitter was probably a high court official; the coins may indicate that he worked for the Mint, or that he was a collector. Bought by Mrs Bambridge in 1949.

JOHN WOOTTON (c.1682–1764)
Prince George of Denmark's 'Leeds'
Sold by Wootton to Lord Harley for 12 gns. Leeds was a celebrated racehorse that Queen Anne gave to her consort, and for which she paid £1,000.

JOHN WOOTTON (c.1682–1764)
The Harlequin bitch 'Casey'
In the 1747 Welbeck catalogue called 'A Harlequin bitch (Casey) on a Cushion, with a Picture as in the room of Mina and Die, two other Dogs'. Wootton's very unusual portrayal of the spaniel, Mina, and the greyhound, Die, in the overmantel is part of the joke of painting Casey as grandly as if she were her mistress, Lady Harley.

JOHN WOOTTON (c.1682–1764)
A Wolf
Wolves had been exterminated in England by the eighteenth century, so this animal was evidently in the Menagerie at Wimpole. The unconvincing characterisation suggests that Wootton was working from a corpse.

JOHN WOOTTON (c.1682–1764)
An Antelope
Wootton charged Lord Harley 10 gns for this picture in 1720. It is one of a pair of 'antelopes'

The Entrance Hall

(actually Indian Blackbuck) from Bengal given to Lord Harley in 1719 by Robert Williamson. Also perhaps painted from a corpse.

FURNITURE

Pair of English carved pine console tables with marble tops, decorated with rams' heads and swags of flowers. On them stands a pair of urns.
Three black and gilt painted cane-backed armchairs, late eighteenth century.
Luggage trunk belonging to Rudyard Kipling.
Mahogany wine-cooler with ormolu decoration, used as a planter.
A pair of painted cane-backed English armchairs, late eighteenth century.
Leather-covered hall porter's chair, late eighteenth century.

CLOCKS

Small, eight-day striking spring clock in mahogany case with a pagoda top, by Peter Nordsteen, c.1780. Nordsteen worked both in Russia and Sweden.
Mahogany longcase clock with an eight-day striking movement by George Stephenson of Warminster, c.1830. Rocking automata ship in the arch above the dial.

THE ANTE ROOM

This formed the south-west corner of the Chicheley house. It was used in the twentieth century by Mrs Bambridge as a drawing-room.

DECORATION

The panelling and neo-Palladian doorcases were installed by Flitcroft in the 1740s. The decorative carving is believed to be the work of Sefferin Alken, who was paid £600 from the 1st Lord Hardwicke at this period. The ceiling, a striking pastiche of eighteenth-century plasterwork, was added by Kendall in the 1840s. The survival of gilded filletting here and in other rooms where Kendall worked suggests that in the nineteenth century many of the walls were hung with silk. The present colour scheme, buff walls with cream panels and pale blue mouldings, was devised by the Trust in the 1970s.

PICTURES

(Clockwise from the far door.)

MEYNIKE (fl.1770s)
An officer of the Hungarian Life Guards from front and back
Pastel.

Inscribed on the backing-paper: *Meÿnike pinx.*
The Corps of Hungarian Life Guards was formed by the Empress Maria Theresa, and dissolved in 1918. According to Sacheverell Sitwell's *Valse des Fleurs*, they were 'the *ne plus ultra* of the hussar'. Recorded at Wimpole in 1880, so perhaps a Hardwicke picture not removed.

JEAN-MAXIME CLAUDE, known as MAX CLAUDE (1824–1904)
Riders sheltering under Constitution Arch
Panel.
Signed bottom right: *J. Max. Claude 1872/London.*
Until 1883 Decimus Burton's Constitution Arch (1827–8), which was intended as the northern entrance to Buckingham Palace, was aligned with his Ionic Screen to Hyde Park (1824–5).

PIERRE-ALEXANDRE WILLE (1748–1821)
Les étrennes de Julie
Signed lower r.: *P. A. Wille filius pxit./1783 no. 72.*
The letter is addressed to 'Mademoiselle Julie', the heroine of Rousseau's *La nouvelle Heloïse* (1761), of which this picture appears to be a somewhat fanciful illustration. Exhibited in the 1783 Salon.

Manner of JAN BRUEGHEL I (1568–1625)
A garden scene
Panel.
A wholly unpeopled landscape or garden is rare in Netherlandish painting. Indeed, two figures (Vertumnus and Pomona) were painted out before the picture was bought by Mrs Bambridge.

ENGLISH, 19th century
Fashionable company, with a coach and a maypole
Panel.
Discrepancies of style and costume suggest that this is a later pastiche.

ALEXANDER RITTER VON BENSA (1820–1902)
A four-in-hand driving through a wood
Board.
Signed bottom right: *A. de Bensa.*
The 'chevalier de Bensa' was self-taught, and only took to painting later in life. He specialised in military scenes, and was particularly patronised by the Austrian Imperial family.

JOHANN GEORG BÖHM THE ELDER (1672/3–1746)
Minerva chastising Cupid for disrupting the Arts
Panel.
Signed bottom right: *J. G. Böhm/inv. f.*
The Arts that Cupid has been disturbing are all being practised by young pupils, including two girls, one (symbolising Geometry) taking measurements on a globe, and the other – very unusually in this context – working at an embroidery frame. Böhm made the first German translation of Leonardo's *Treatise on Painting* (1724). Bought by Capt. Bambridge in 1942.

FLEMISH, *c.*1780–90
Figures promenading in front of a palace
A rather naïve depiction in the manner of Watteau de Lille (1731–98), perhaps set in the Austrian Netherlands. Bought by Capt. Bambridge in 1936.

CLÉMENT-AUGUSTE ANDRIEUX (1829–after 1880)
A girl smoking
Watercolour.
Signed bottom left: *Andrieux.*
Andrieux was best known for his watercolours and lithographs of everyday and military scenes.

(?) RICHARD PARKES BONINGTON (1801–28)
'The Use of Tears' or *'The Love-Sick Maid'*
Watercolour.
Signed (?) bottom centre: *Bonnington pinx.*
Apparently, Bonington's own reduction of his very similar oil painting (1826–7; Boston, Museum of Fine Arts), and not a copy by another hand. Bought by Joseph Balestier in Paris, *c.*1860–70, and bequeathed to his granddaughter, Caroline Balestier, Mrs Rudyard Kipling.

GEORGE CARTER (1737–94)
Officer of a Sepoy Regiment with his syce and a drummer
Signed lower right: *G. Carter pinx. 1786.*
One of only two pictures by the peripatetic Carter known to date from his stay in India, 1786–7. 'Syce' was the Anglo-Indian term for groom.

(?) PIETER CASTEELS (1684–1749)
Peacock and chickens, with the view of a house
Signed(?) bottom right: *P. Casteels f./1731* [?]
The Bambridges probably bought this picture because the house resembled Wimpole.

EDWARD SMITH (fl. *c.*1740–73)
An angling party
Transcribed signature on lining canvas:
Ed. Smith/at Fowy/Cornwall. inv. & Pinx'./1773.
Possibly a portrait of the Willyams family outside their Cornish mansion, Carnanton, before its nineteenth-century transformation. Bought by Capt. Bambridge from the Arthur Gilbey Collection of Angling Pictures.

WILLIAM PARROT (dates unknown)
A fishing scene
Watercolour.
Signed bottom left: *William Parrot.*
Too early (*c.*1830) and too amateur to be the William Parrot (1813–69) who painted Continental scenes in oils and watercolours. Bought by Capt. Bambridge in the Gilbey sale.

Attributed to DAVID COX (1783–1859)
Lancaster Sands
Oil on paper laid down on mill-board.
Lancaster Sands (also called Ulverston Sands) extend between Lancaster and Ulverston at the head of Morecambe Bay. David Cox visited Lancaster and the Sands in 1834, 1835 and 1840, where, inspired by Turner, he produced numerous oil sketches and watercolours, of which this may, however, be an imitation.

(?) ENGLISH, 19th century
Sketch of a French commander before an arch
The horseman is dressed in military costume of the mid-eighteenth century; the star and blue sash probably belong to the Order of the Saint-Esprit.

ALEXANDER RITTER VON BENSA (1820–1902)
Carriages in a Park
Board.
Signed bottom right: *A Bensa.*
The pendant to his picture of the four-in-hand.

ARTHUR DEVIS (1711/12–87)
Portrait of an Unknown Couple
Signed on the tree-trunk: *A. Devis fe./174(?)*
The offering of honeysuckle, a symbol of endearment, indicates that this unknown couple are man and wife. Bought by Capt. Bambridge in 1940 as a portrait of Horace Walpole and Kitty Clive.

AUSTRIAN, *c.*1770
The Empress Maria Theresa as a widow
Indistinctly signed and dated.
Maria Theresa (1717–80), who lost her husband, the Emperor Francis I, in 1765, is shown as a widow in a park, adorned with the medal of the Innsbruck Damenstift, which she founded to commemorate her widowhood. She never left off wearing her widow's weeds.

FURNITURE
Rosewood writing-table with a *trompe l'oeil* painting of cards, coins and documents (including a sonata of 1774 by Charpentier) on its upper surface,

'Trompe l'oeil' painted table-top by L. Boilly, 1774 (Ante Room)

signed by L. Boilly (1761–1845). Boilly is best known for his meticulous scenes of Paris life in the late eighteenth and early nineteenth centuries. His father was a woodcarver in Lille and it is possible that this is an early work produced under his father's influence. Boilly certainly produced *trompe l'oeil* paintings, but this example appears to be unique, and the signature may not be genuine. The legs may also be later.
Pair of painted cane-back armchairs, English, late eighteenth century.
Sheraton-style mahogany and satinwood serpentine-fronted card-table.
Sheraton-style rosewood and satinwood semi-circular side-table.
Lacquered work-table.
French, mahogany *bureau à cylindre.*
Walnut chair with caned back, from the Provence region of France.

55

Rococo revival giltwood pier-glass, mid-nineteenth century.

Giltwood console table with marbled top, mid-nineteenth century.

CERAMICS

LEFT-HAND CORNER CUPBOARD

A selection of English figures, including a group of masked dancers, Chelsea c.1755, based on the Meissen Dutch or Tyrolean dancers modelled by J. F. Eberlein in 1735. Loosely based on the Meissen *Commedia dell'Arte* are the two early Bow figures of the Harlequin and the Captain, c.1750.

Bow sportswoman similar to pair of Meissen figures of a sportsman and companion, modelled by Eberlein, c.1745, in the other case.

Rare Chelsea gold anchor figure of a negro, c.1765, and the Longton Hall group of a putto on horseback, c.1755.

Derby figures of June and a fisherman, c.1765 and c.1770.

RIGHT-HAND CORNER CUPBOARD

An interesting selection of Continental porcelain figures collected by Mrs Bambridge, the most important being the Nymphenburg figure of the Abbé or Anselmo, one of the sixteen characters from the *Commedia dell'Arte*, modelled by Franz Anton Bustelli. With the three figures in the Gubbay Collection at Clandon Park in Surrey, and the figure of Scaramouche at Fenton House in London, the National Trust has the most important collection of these Bavarian rococo figures in Britain.

Girl with a muff, Berlin, c.1755.

Unusual figures from Thuringia, Höchst, Ludwigsburg, Naples and Meissen. The most amusing of the Meissen figures is of The Courtesan modelled by Peter Reinicke in 1757 after a sketch by Christophe Huet for the *Cris de Paris*.

BRONZES

ON THE MANTELPIECE

Four busts representing the Continents, French.

CARPET

Tekke rug from central Asia.

THE SOUTH DRAWING ROOM

Extending beyond the earlier house, this room forms the first part of the west wing added by Gibbs between 1713 and 1721. Remodelled by Flitcroft and in turn by Kendall, its arrangement reflects Mrs Bambridge's taste.

DECORATION

Like that in the Ante Room, the ceiling and cornice plasterwork was executed by the Cambridge firm of Rattee and Kett to the design of Kendall, c.1842. The panelling and doorcases, also identical to those in the Ante Room, are the work of Flitcroft. The cream and buff colour scheme matches that in the Ante Room.

FIREPLACE

The carved wooden surround and overmantel are probably the work of Sefferin Alken, who also worked for Flitcroft at Stourhead in Wiltshire, and at Milton in Northamptonshire. Decorated with the mask of Flora.

PICTURES

(Clockwise, beginning at the far door.)

BRITISH, 1829
Apotheosis of the Royal Family
Indistinctly signed: *PAINTED by . . . Briton[?] 1829*
This picture depicts Britannia mourning the deceased members of George IV's family, and their reunion in heaven: George III (d.1820), carrying the two young princes who died in infancy, Octavius (d.1783) and Alfred (d.1782), rises to meet Queen Charlotte (d.1818); behind him are their sons, the Dukes of York (d.1827) and Kent (d.1820); above her are their daughters, Charlotte, Queen of Württemberg (d.1828), and Amelia (d.1810), with to the left George IV's repudiated Queen, Caroline (d.1821); beside her, her daughter by George IV, Princess Charlotte, and the still-born child she died giving birth to (d.1817).

JOHN DOWNMAN (1750–1824)
Lady Mary Somerset, Duchess of Rutland (d.1831)
Chalk and wash.
Signed lower right: *J. Downman/D'. 1783.*
Lady Mary Isabella was the youngest daughter of the 4th Duke of Beaufort, and married the 4th Duke of Rutland in 1775. Bought by Capt. Bambridge from the Gilbey Collection.

The South Drawing Room

PHILIP MERCIER (1689/91–1760)
A young woman with a bottle and a glass
The sitter was described as a 'nymph' in the eighteenth century, and hence perhaps was from the *demi-monde*. Bought with its companion by Mrs Bambridge in 1957. The painting is badly abraded.

TILLY KETTLE (1735–86)
Master George Graham (1771–1832)
Painted in 1774 in India, it shows the son of John Graham, of the Supreme Council of Bengal. George Graham became a colonel in the Sussex militia and MP for Kinross. He ultimately lived at Abington Pigotts, Cambridgeshire, which may have stimulated the Bambridges to buy this picture. Kettle painted seven portraits of the Graham family.

PHILIP MERCIER (1689/91–1760)
A young woman with a patch box
The pendant to *A young woman with a bottle and a glass*.

NICOLAS MAES (1634–93)
Portrait of a girl as Venus in her chariot
Signed bottom left: *N MAES*.

It was quite common in Holland in the seventeenth century to portray sitters in mythological guises, regardless of incongruity. Bought by Capt. Bambridge in 1940.

Manner of HENRY TRESHAM (1750/1–1814)
A boating party of the Prince of Wales
The Prince of Wales (later George IV), in the centre, gazes ardently at his mistress, Mrs Fitzherbert, with whom he lived from 1785 to 1803; to the left are the playwright Richard Brinsley Sheridan and a woman labelled as 'Miss Stephens' (probably an anachronistic identification with the singer who became Countess of Essex); in front, Elizabeth

Linley, Mrs Sheridan (d.1792), and Jacob Pleydell-Bouverie, 2nd Earl of Radnor. The scene is probably an allegory of the reconciliation effected by Sheridan between Mrs Fitzherbert and the Prince of Wales in 1787, after Fox had disavowed their marriage to Parliament, apparently on the authority of the Prince, to ensure that the settlement of the latter's debts was voted through. Once owned by the Sheridan family.

THOMAS HICKEY (1741–1824)
Lady Newcomen (1747/8–1817) with her daughters in a garden
Charlotte Newcomen of Carrickglas, Co. Longford, married around 1770 William Gleadowe of Killester, Co. Dublin, who added the name of Newcomen to his own, was made a baronet in 1781 and died in 1807. 'In consideration of her husband's services' in promoting the Union, she was created Baroness in the Irish peerage in 1800, and Viscountess in 1803. Of her three daughters, Jane, Theresa and Charlotte, Theresa married Sir Charles Turner of Kirkleatham. Her only son, the last Viscount, was not born until 1776. Probably painted by Hickey between his return from Italy in 1767 and his departure to India in 1780.

ELIOT THOMAS YORKE, MP, DL (1805–85)
The Great Avenue of Wimpole from the Terrace
Watercolour.
The Great Avenue of elms to the south of the house, extending for 2 miles, was planted by Charles Bridgeman in the 1720s, but destroyed by Dutch elm disease in the 1970s. The artist was the third son of Vice-Admiral Sir Joseph Yorke. Bought in 1982.

FURNITURE

Painted and gilded, circular-topped tripod table, by Peter Tune, 1930.
Pair of Austrian painted cupboards, c.1750–70.
Austrian painted and gilded display cabinet, mid-eighteenth century.
Italian side-table, marble top, mid-eighteenth century.
Pair of small pillar tables with parquetry tops, Regency.
Three French painted armchairs, late eighteenth century.
Austrian painted and gilded, carved side-table, with pierced frieze and marbled top, mid-eighteenth century.

Austrian painted and gilded commode with pierced apron and ormolu fittings, eighteenth century.
Pair of painted French armchairs, mid-eighteenth century.
Pair of Rococo revival giltwood pier-glasses. Possibly nineteenth century.
Pair of gilt console tables with marbled tops, early nineteenth century.

CERAMICS AND ORNAMENTS

DISPLAY CABINET
It contains eighteenth-century Worcester porcelain, brown and gold anchor marked Chelsea plates, a Worcester candlestick and other pieces painted in the style of William Doe, and modern Nymphenburg figures in the eighteenth-century Frankenthal style.
Four, two-handled vases, one pair decorated with Chinese birds, the other with panels of figures on a blue ground.
Chelsea white bust of George III as Prince of Wales, c.1751–2, possibly inspired by a sculpture by Roubiliac.
Pierced basket, Paris porcelain, c.1800.

CARPET

Aubusson, nineteenth century.

THE GALLERY

Built as a series of three cabinets by Gibbs, c.1716, in order to house Lord Harley's collections of coins, antiquities, manuscripts and curiosities. In 1742 it was opened up by Flitcroft to form a single room. Flitcroft's instructions to the joiner, c.1744, specified: 'New Pedestall, doors and bracket for plaister cornice and four Ionick Collumns and four Pillasters with Entablatures over them.' Its new function was as a picture gallery where Lord Chancellor Hardwicke hung the best of his Old Master paintings. Soane's survey shows that by 1790 a third, central column had been added to strengthen Flitcroft's two Ionic screens. The present columns were probably inserted by Kendall in the last century.

DECORATION

The Italian stuccatore, Giuseppe Artari, who worked at Wimpole with Flitcroft, was probably responsible for the decorative plasterwork of the wall-panels. The ceiling plasterwork is again pastiche of the 1840s; it was redecorated in a simple blue-green in the 1970s after investigative paint scrapes. The red damask curtains, hung as part of the redecoration, are reefed in the manner described in a letter to Lady Hardwicke from one of her daughters, Lady Anson, in 1750.

FIREPLACE

White Carrara marble chimney-piece, its frieze decorated with the mask of Bacchus and festoons of vines, probably carved by Peter Scheemakers, who worked on three of the monuments in the church between 1759 and 1770. The wooden overmantel may be attributed to Sefferin Alken. Polished steel grate, nineteenth century.

PICTURES

(Clockwise, beginning with the overmantel.)

(?) JOHN WOOTTON (c.1682–1764)
A staghunt in full cry
Contrary to appearances, this Wootton is not an indigenous overmantel, but was acquired by Mrs Bambridge in 1959. Its poor condition makes it impossible to establish whether it is autograph.

(?) Sir PETER LELY (1618–80)
(?) Mrs (later Lady) Chicheley, née Lawson
Most probably the daughter of one of Lely's 'Flaggmen', Sir John Lawson. She was noticed as 'very pretty' by Pepys in 1666, the year in which she lost her first husband, Mr Norton. Probably in the following year she married John Chicheley, son of Sir Thomas, with whose wife the sitter was previously identified.

THOMAS HUDSON (1701–79)
Catherine Freman, the Hon. Mrs Charles Yorke
(d.1759)
Daughter and heiress of William Freman of Aspeden and Catherine Blount of Tittenhanger (both Hertfordshire); married to the Hon. Charles Yorke, as his first wife, in 1755, when this portrait was probably painted. Bought at the Earl of Hardwicke's sale in 1967.

THOMAS HUDSON (1701–79)
The Hon. Charles Yorke (1722–70)
Second son of the 1st Earl of Hardwicke, married first (1755) to Catherine Freman, and secondly (1762) to Agneta Johnston. Appointed Solicitor-General in 1756, Attorney-General in 1765, and Lord Chancellor (like his father before him) in 1770, but died on the day after his acceptance of the appointment. Although bought by Mrs Bambridge along with the portrait of Yorke's wife, it is far from certain that they are pendants (and they are not framed so). This picture was probably painted to

The Gallery

celebrate the sitter's appointment as Solicitor-General in 1756.

FRANCIS COTES (1726–70)
Sir William Jones, Bt (d.1791)
Signed lower left: *F Cotes R:A:px./1769.*
William Jones (formerly Langham) was made a baronet in 1774. He took the name of Jones after his marriage to Elizabeth, sister and coheiress of William Jones of Ramsbury Manor, Wiltshire. It was bought by Mrs Bambridge in 1960, apparently in the mistaken belief that the sitter was the son-in-law of the mathematician of the same name, who had been tutor and friend to the 1st Earl of Hardwicke.

JONATHAN RICHARDSON Senior (1664/5–1745)
(?) George Vertue (1683–1756)
Recorded at Wimpole, as one of the Hardwicke collection of historical portraits, in 1880. Then wrongly considered a portrait of the 2nd Earl of Oxford's great friend, the poet and diplomat Matthew Prior, it closely resembles Richardson's head-and-shoulders of the connoisseur George Vertue (1733; National Portrait Gallery). The mistake is not an unhappy one, since Vertue also 'greatly shar'd [the Earl's] favour, protection and honour', made half-a-dozen tours of country houses with him, and catalogued his pictures after his death.

ALLAN RAMSAY (1713–84)
Lady Jemima Campbell, Marchioness Grey, Countess of Hardwicke (c.1720–97)
Signed on the plinth: *A. Ramsay 1741* and inscribed (before 1752) with the sitter's identity.
Lady Jemima was daughter of John, Lord Glenorchy (later 3rd Earl of Breadalbane), and of Lady Amabel de Grey, daughter and co-heir of Henry, Duke of Kent, whom she succeeded as Marchionesss Grey in 1740. In the same year she married the Hon. Philip Yorke, later 2nd Earl of Hardwicke; they had two daughters, Amabel and Mary, but no son.

Attributed to JOHN HAYLS (fl.1641–79)
Portrait wrongly said to be of Sir Thomas Chicheley (1618–99)
Bought by Mrs Bambridge around 1957 as a portrait of Sir Thomas Chicheley, the spendthrift builder and alienator of the first house at Wimpole. There is, however, no resemblance to Sir Thomas as he is shown in Dobson's sure portrait of him (private collection), and the sitter is much younger than Sir Thomas would have been in the 1640s, when this portrait was painted.

SCULPTURE
Plaster bust of Newton after Rysbrack, by P. Sarti, of Dean Street, Soho.

FURNITURE
Pair of elaborately carved giltwood console tables with a central lion's mask and green marble tops, mid-eighteenth century.
Two giltwood pier glasses with original glass, mid-eighteenth century. Both console tables and pier glasses may well have been here since 1742, when Flitcroft opened up the Gallery.
Two gilded and painted side-tables with marble tops, probably nineteenth-century in the style of William Kent.
Gilded and painted side-table, the apron carved with the mask of Hercules draped with a lion's pelt, probably mid-eighteenth century. This table is similar to a drawing by Matthias Lock in the Victoria and Albert Museum.

CERAMICS
Pair of long-necked Imari vases, nineteenth century.
Pair of blue and white Chinese vases, nineteenth century.

CARPET
Persian Sultanabad carpet, twentieth century.

MUSICAL INSTRUMENTS
Boudoir Grand Pianoforte by Blüthner of Leipzig, 1902. Finished largely in Brazilian rosewood.

THE BOOK ROOM

In 1730 Gibbs annexed the two easternmost bays from Lord Radnor's orangery to form a square ante-room to Lord Harley's new Library wing. The design of the eastern section of the coved ceiling corresponds to a drawing by Gibbs in the Ashmolean Museum, Oxford. The plasterwork here has been attributed to Isaac Mansfield.

In 1806, by incorporating a further two bays of the orangery, Soane doubled the size of the room to accommodate the 3rd Earl of Hardwicke's additional books. Elliptical arches, decorated with plaster *paterae*, spring from bookcases projecting into the room, and support a barrel-vaulted ceiling. The *paterae*, ceiling plaster and plaster urns in the arched recesses above the bookcases are the work of

(Opposite page) The Book Room

the plasterer John Papworth. Until the boiler house, which ran along the west side of the Library, was demolished, presumably in the 1950s, at the same time as the Kendall wings, there were double doors in the north-west corner of the room leading into it. There was also access to the cellars at this point. French windows at the west end of the room originally led into the remainder of Lord Radnor's orangery, remodelled first by Humphry Repton in 1809, and subsequently by Kendall in 1870, some thirty years after he had designed it and the east service wing. Kendall's orangery ended in an apse, and its glazed roof was supported on neo-Jacobean hammerbeam trusses. Facsimiles of Kendall's water-colours of this building hang in the Breakfast Room. The doors now lead directly into the garden.

FIREPLACE

The chimney-piece and dramatic, gilded over-mantel mirror with pair of three-armed sconces were designed by Soane. The marble chimney-piece was supplied by the mason James Nelson.

SCULPTURE

NEAR DOOR TO LIBRARY
Plaster bust of the great eighteenth-century actor David Garrick, finished to resemble Wedgwood black basaltes ware fashionable from the 1770s, like the urns above the bookcases.

ON CENTRAL TABLE
Plaster caricature of the French statesman Talley-rand, by Dantan, 1833.

FURNITURE

Mahogany partner's desk, late eighteenth century.
Mahogany dumb-waiter, with swivelling shelves on turned supports, Regency.
Central pillar mahogany breakfast-table, Regency.
Suite of black and gilt painted sabre-leg dining-chairs with cane seats, Regency.

CLOCK

Marble and ormolu mantel clock with an eight-day quarter striking movement by Robert Courvoisier of Geneva, c.1800.

THE LIBRARY

This magnificent room, almost a double cube, was designed by Gibbs in order to house Lord Harley's vast collection of books (50,000) and pamphlets (350,000); it was completed in 1730. There are sketch designs for the arcaded bookcases, and a drawing for the ceiling by Gibbs in the Ashmolean Museum. The ceiling plasterwork is attributed to Isaac Mansfield, who also worked with Gibbs at the Senate House in Cambridge, while much of the freehand 'decoration' is thought to be by the Italian plasterer Bagutti. Originally the fireplace stood at the north end of the room, which was lit solely by five windows in the east wall, the west wall being entirely lined with bookcases. In c.1754 the 1st Earl of Hardwicke blocked three of the windows, moved the chimney-piece to its present position at the centre of the west wall, and added the bay window at the north end. This work has been attributed to the architect Sanderson Miller, but it may have been carried out by Henry Flitcroft; the carved pilasters, with lions' masks and garlands of flowers, which flank the bay window are identical to the work in the Saloon by Flitcroft's collab-orator, Sefferin Alken. Mrs Bambridge inserted two further windows in the west wall, which resulted in the loss of book presses D and G.

FIREPLACE

Overmantel mirror in the Aesthetic taste. In the 1940s this hung on the west wall of Kendall's State Dining Room, above the Hercules-mask side-table now in the Gallery.

SCULPTURE

ON CENTRAL TABLE
Ivory bust of Lord Chancellor Somers, by David Le Marchand, 1706.

FURNITURE

Mahogany arch-topped chest, eighteenth century.
Pair of mahogany circular hall tables with ormolu mounts and marble tops, Regency.
Oak pulpit inlaid with Gothick tracery in walnut and mounted on castors to serve as library stairs. The architect Henry Keene's designs for the pulpit are in the Victoria and Albert Museum.
Pair of globes, one terrestrial, one celestial, by William Cary, early nineteenth century.
Four mahogany library chairs in George II style.

Reproduction mahogany drum-top table.

Four leather-covered library chairs, nineteenth century.

Arch-topped lacquered chest on painted stand, mid-eighteenth century.

CARPET

The eighteenth-century English carpet is probably an Axminster. The shell, palm fronds and garlands of flowers on a chocolate ground perfectly complement the ceiling plasterwork and the restrained colour scheme of the room as a whole, although it is thought to have been made for another house and is certainly too large for its present position.

THE RED ROOM

Built as part of Gibbs's additions of 1713–21, it is the mirror image of the South Drawing Room. The doorcases are again survivals of Flitcroft's work in the 1740s, and the ceiling (again in an early eighteenth-century manner) is by Kendall of 1842. Used as a family dining-room until 1939, Mrs Bambridge subsequently catalogued and stored her father's papers here. In 1978 the National Trust deposited the Kipling papers, on permanent loan, in the Library of the University of Sussex, which is close to Kipling's own home at Bateman's (also a National Trust property). The room now contains a display of drawings by the architects and landscape designers who shaped Wimpole, and an exhibition of archaeological finds associated with the estate.

DECORATION

Redecorated in 'Pompeian' colours over a late nineteenth-century 'Lincrusta' wallpaper.

FIREPLACE

White marble chimney-piece, carved with vines and bunches of grapes. Inserted by Soane.

PICTURE

THOMAS PHILLIPS (1770–1845)
Philip Yorke, 3rd Earl of Hardwicke (1757–1834)
The 3rd Earl is shown in the robes of the Order of the Garter, of which he was dubbed Knight in 1813. It was he who employed Soane to make the house at Wimpole into a coherent whole, and Repton to transform the park. Bought at the Earl of Hardwicke's sale by the NA-CF for the Trust in 1979.

FURNITURE

Pair of ebony display cabinets with brass inlays and ormolu mounts, mid-nineteenth century.

Series of painted beechwood shield-back chairs, pierced splat with Prince of Wales plumes, George III.

Pair of black and gilt console tables, Regency.

Pair of ornate giltwood console tables in the form of trees inhabited by birds, with marble tops, nineteenth century.

THE BACK STAIRCASE

Designed by Soane as part of his Yellow Drawing Room scheme of 1793, and built in the inner courtyard left between Gibbs's west wing and the seventeenth-century house. The ironwork of the stair balustrade, typical of Soane's work, was supplied by the London smith J. Mackell. The glass of the large skylight, made by Cox & Co., was originally painted with heraldic motifs, of which only a fragment survives. There is evidence within the later glazed superstructure that gas lighting may have been used to show off the glass by night. An inventory of 1835 refers to a pedestal stove in the basement which was used to warm the west staircase and whose pipe, presumably rising through the centre of the stair-well, exited from the skylight.

DECORATION

Redecorated in 1988 in the colours of the original scheme.

PICTURE

JOHN WOOTTON (c.1682–1764)
The Dun Arabian with an eastern attendant.
Painted by 1720 for Lord Harley for 25 guineas.

CLOCK

Eight-day 'Regulator' clock in a glazed mahogany case, from the Comptoise area of north-west France, c.1850.

THE YELLOW DRAWING ROOM

A remarkable T-shaped room, created by Soane in 1793 for the 3rd Earl of Hardwicke, in order to display the gems of his picture collection and to provide the grand reception room for staging county balls and concerts which Wimpole had hitherto lacked. Soane's first suggestion, of adding a bow front to the Saloon and incorporating the Red Room and Breakfast Room to either side, was rejected because it would have disrupted the garden façade. His final solution was ingenious and original. The double-height space, with its 'nave' and apsidal 'transepts', was formed by removing the divisions between three of the ground-floor rooms, which included the seventeenth-century service staircase, and four first-floor rooms. The design of the room was then worked out on almost ecclesiastical lines, using the chimney-piece as an 'altar', with a wide skylight dome over the 'crossing', and 'transepts' in the form of semi-circular apses either side. From any angle the result is intensely dramatic, and there is no doubt that this ranks as the finest of all his country-house interiors.

DECORATION

A mixture of Neo-classical motifs derived from William Chambers, and more strictly archaeological details derived from the treatises of Le Roy, Durand and others. Many of the motifs in the plasterwork, the work of John Papworth, are repeated elsewhere in the house. A watercolour by Soane in the Soane Museum shows the walls hung with yellow silk panels with blue borders, separated by black panels apparently painted with white arabesques. The room was redecorated in the 1840s, and again in 1898, when the walls were papered with a gold and silver 'Lincrusta' paper. This was replaced by the present yellow silk panels, which were woven for Mrs Bambridge in 1963, the fabric copied from the original curtains.

FIREPLACE

Carved marble chimney-piece supplied by the mason James Nelson; its Vitruvian foliage scroll motif is echoed both in the carved wooden surrounds to the two mirrors and in the ceiling plasterwork. The polished steel grate and fender were supplied by the ironmongers Bickley and Lordner.

LIGHTING

Soane solved the problem of lighting the room, immured as it is at the heart of the building, by placing a lantern, rising up between the front and rear roofs of the original, double-pile house, over an oculus at the centre of the domed ceiling. While he was dismissive of top-lit rooms for domestic use, Soane did point out in one of his Royal Academy lectures that 'in extensive magnificent houses opportunities will occur of introducing them with great talent'. Soane's inclusion of two large mirrors, the lower part of that at the northern end decorated with gilt balusters that echo the stone ones outside, and his choice of yellow silk for the walls must have been central to the lighting effect he wished to achieve. The room would have been seen most often by candlelight.

In 1816 Soane supervised the installation of gas lighting into his similarly domed halls in the Bank of England, and it is possible that he had a say in choosing the crystal gasolier in the dome, which resembles those used in the Bank and was fuelled directly from the estate gasworks. The lighting of inaccessible lamps was made possible with the discovery by the German scientist Johann Wolfgang Döbereiner, that gas ignites automatically when passed over a black platinum nipple; he sold 2,000 such devices in England, and the Yellow Drawing Room gasolier may have been lit in this way. The controls regulating the flow of gas can be seen in the Inner Hall.

PICTURES

OVERDOORS

JOHN CRACE
Allegories of Poetry, Painting, Music and Drama
Four grisailles, *c*.1790.

LUNETTES
ROBERT WILLIAM BUSS (1804–74)
The Origin of Music and *The Triumph of Music*, *c*.1845
They depict assemblies of the gods as playing *amorini*, including several portraits of the 4th Earl of Hardwicke's children.

WILLIAM ASHFORD (*c*.1746–1824)
Landscape with a triumphal arch: Morning
Signed bottom left: *W. Ashford 1777*.
Ashford had a job in the Ordnance Office in Dublin from 1764 until 1788, but from 1772 onwards practised increasingly as a landscape-painter, both in the idealising Claudian mode – as here – and in a more factual, topographical vein. Acquired by Mrs Bambridge around 1965.

(Opposite page) The Yellow Drawing Room

WILLIAM ASHFORD (c.1746–1824)
Landscape with Mercury and Argus: Evening
Signed bottom left: *W. Ashford 1777.*
Pendant to the above, but more Salvator Rosa-ish in inspiration. Mercury was sent by Jupiter to lull the hundred-eyed Argus to sleep with his piping, so that he could cut off the beast's head and release Jupiter's beloved Io. Jupiter had transformed Io into a cow in the vain hope of sheltering her from the jealous anger of his wife, Juno.

GEORGE ROMNEY (1734–1802)
Lady Elizabeth Lindsay, Countess of Hardwicke (d.1858)
The youngest daughter of the 5th Earl of Balcarres and Anne Dalrymple married the future 3rd Earl of Hardwicke in 1782, just before which a single sitting with Romney is recorded. A black dress was subsequently painted on, probably after the Countess had lost both her sons in quick succession: Philip (b.1784) in 1808, and Charles James (b.1797) in 1810. Mrs Bambridge had it removed when she bought the picture.

GEORGE ROMNEY (1734–1802)
Philip Yorke, 3rd Earl of Hardwicke (1757–1834)
Romney painted two 'Kit-cat' portraits – half-length with hands – of the Hon. Philip Yorke. This one is in the pose of an Eton or Harrow leaving-portrait. From the mid-eighteenth century it became customary for boys leaving these schools to present a portrait to their headmaster instead of a gratuity; unlike Eton portraits, those at Harrow were returned on the death of the recipient. Bought by Mrs Bambridge in 1946.

HENRI-PIERRE DANLOUX (1753–1809)
Harriott Manningham, Mrs Charles Yorke
Old label on the back: *Painted by Danloux circa AD 1793 aetat. 30.*
The sitter was the daughter of Charles Manningham, and in 1790 married Charles Philip Yorke, but had no issue. Painted while Danloux was a refugee in England from the French Revolution. Bought by Capt. Bambridge in 1940.

GEORGE ROMNEY (1734–1802)
Charles Philip Yorke (1764–1834)
Step-brother of the 3rd Earl of Hardwicke, one of the Tellers of the Exchequer and, from 1810 to 1812, First Lord of the Admiralty. This is probably the Harrow leaving-portrait that the sitter is recorded as giving to the headmaster in 1779. Bought by Capt. Bambridge in 1940.

FURNITURE

Two giltwood, semi-circular side-tables with marble tops. Suite of six giltwood settees (four curved to fit the walls of the 'transepts'), and eight armchairs, made for the room, c.1793. The craftsmen responsible are unknown, but the furniture is similar to that made for Shugborough by the Royal Upholsterers, Charles Smith and Co., of Lower Grosvenor Street, London.
Four torchères of very similar design, two bought by Mrs Bambridge in the 1950s and two copied for her.

CARPET

Red Axminster, late nineteenth century, with an earlier blue and gold border (c.1845) incorporating a monogram and coronet.

THE SALOON

The room at the centre of the north front in the seventeenth-century house was asymmetrical. Flitcroft created the present room for the 1st Earl of Hardwicke in 1745 by extending its predecessor to the east by one bay, and by adding the bay window to the north. Throughout the nineteenth century it was used as a billiards room; the 1835 inventory lists the furniture associated with the game.

DECORATION

The oak-grained window surrounds, shutters, doorcases, carved overmantel, and the brackets flanking the bay window with their lion's mask panels below (as in the Library), are presumably the work of Sefferin Alken and his assistants. The marble chimney-piece has been attributed to Peter Scheemakers. The ceiling was added by Kendall.

PICTURES

(?) JACOB BOGDANI (c.1660–1724) and
(?) JAN VAN DER VAART (1653–1727)
Flowers in an urn, with a boy feeding two parrots
Evidently the work of two hands, one a specialist painter of flowers in elaborate vessels and settings in the manner of Monnoyer, possibly the Hungarian, Bogdani, and the face by a professional portrait-painter, possibly the Dutchman, van der Vaart. Van der Vaart was used to collaboration from his earliest work with Wissing. Painted *c*.1700. Bought by Capt. Bambridge in 1940.

Sir Joshua Reynolds (1723–92)
Elizabeth Dashwood, Duchess of Manchester, as Diana disarming Cupid (her son, George, Vt Mandeville)
Reynolds's first entry to the first Royal Academy exhibition in 1769, and thus something of a manifesto of his art. In borrowing the motif and the pose from Francesco Albani's *Disarming of Cupid* (Paris, Louvre), Reynolds considered he was exploiting the Old Masters creatively to raise the status of portraiture, but he was attacked as a plagiarist by Nathaniel Hone in his painting, *The Conjuror* (1775). Horace Walpole's dismissive comment 'bad attitude' is a fair judgement on a curiously laboured composition. The sitters in this much ruined portrait have no connection with Wimpole; Mrs Bambridge probably bought it and the Dupont below purely to furnish two of the panels in this room.

Gainsborough Dupont (1754–97)
Queen Charlotte (1744–1818)
Based on the original by Gainsborough of 1781 (Royal Collection), of which the artist's nephew scraped the mezzotint, and appears to have painted a number of replicas. Bought by Mrs Bambridge in 1958.

Attributed to A. Sijmons (dates unknown)
A group of six manège horses
Commonly said to show the dressage horses of the 1st Duke of Newcastle, whose *Méthode et Invention Nouvelle de Dresser les Chevaux* (Antwerp, 1658) codified the subject. The artist is probably the obscure A. Sijmons, who signed one of three similar and contemporary (*c*.1670) scenes at Welbeck, and not Abraham van Diepenbeke (1596–1675) to whom it has generally been attributed.

SCULPTURE

Basaltes ware head of Mercury.

CISTERN

The marble cistern, similar to a series of plates in James Gibbs's *Book of Architecture* of 1728, is likely to have been designed by him to stand under a dining-room buffet. Its weathered surface is a reflection of the time it has spent as a garden ornament.

FURNITURE

Suite of six oval-backed and five square-backed gilded chairs in French style, from Eaton Hall in Cheshire, the tapestry backs bearing the monogram of its owner, the Duke of Westminster, nineteenth century.
Four ornamental staffs, for footmen.
Billiard cue cupboard.

CLOCKS

English longcase clock in black Chinese lacquer case with eight-day striking movement, by William Kipling of London, *c*.1730.

CARPET

Persian carpet from the Sultanabad (Arak) region, possibly a Ziegler, *c*.1860.

THE INNER HALL

This hall occupies the centre of the Chicheley house. The Ionic columns, designed by Soane and carved by Edward Foxhall, were installed in 1793. Kendall added another more florid pair in the 1840s.

PICTURES

French, 20th century (?)
The Four Seasons represented by Putti
Oval, painted *en camaïeu*.
These half-heartedly illusionistic paintings are adaptations of the reliefs carved on the Fontaine de Grenelle in Paris by Jacques-Edmé Bouchardon, from 1739. Bought by Mrs Bambridge in 1958.

SCULPTURE

Bronzed plaster busts of Locke after Rysbrack, by P. Sarti, and Pitt after Nollekens.

THE GREAT STAIRCASE

The present staircase, inserted by Gibbs between 1720 and 1730, occupies the same position as that in Chicheley's seventeenth-century house. It is lit by four large therm windows in a domed skylight inserted in the 1790s by Soane, who blocked up Flitcroft's large, round-headed window in the east wall in order to build a new service stair beyond. Flitcroft's window, whose margins now frame Kneller's portrait of Bishop Burnet, supplanted two smaller windows inserted by Gibbs.
The finely carved oak balusters, with Corinthian columns as corner posts, are by Gibbs.

'The Warren Hill at Newmarket, with the artist sketching', by John Wootton, 1715 (Great Staircase)

DECORATION

The history of the plasterwork is complex, as it illustrates the consecutive intervention of four architects and their plasterers. The garlands of fruit, flowers and laurel leaves in the coving are a survival of the original seventeenth-century work, comparable to decoration at Wilton in Wiltshire and Coleshill in Berkshire, houses designed by Chicheley's architect friend, Sir Roger Pratt. A drawing in the Ashmolean Museum suggests that Gibbs subsequently inserted a ceiling between the first and second floors, hiding and so protecting Chicheley's work. Gibbs designed and Bagutti probably executed the wall panels containing plasterwork trophies, four of which incorporate medallions of Roman philosophers and orators; Bagutti did similar work at Orleans House, Twickenham. Flitcroft removed Gibbs's ceiling *c*.1742, and built a gallery above the first-floor landing, while Artari, his plasterer, decorated the upper walls with garlands in the Rococo style. The lion's mask and flower garlands beneath the brackets supporting the west gallery are similar to those in the Library and Saloon. The final decoration was added in the 1790s, when Papworth plastered Soane's domed skylight. At the same time Soane added two further upper galleries to the north and south.

PICTURES

JOHN WOOTTON (*c*.1682–1764)
The Watering-Place at Newmarket
The development of Newmarket as a racecourse was begun by James I in 1606, but Wootton and Tillemans, in the eighteenth century, were the first artists to paint the racing there. Painted by Wootton for Lord Harley for £15.

JOHN WOOTTON (*c*.1682–1764)
Landscape with a rivulet and philosophers
Wootton's reputation amongst virtuosi was particularly based upon his ideal landscapes, because of their classical associations. This one, thought to have been painted in the 1720s, is a hybrid of Dughet and Salvator Rosa.

JOHN WOOTTON (*c*.1682–1764)
The Warren Hill at Newmarket, with the artist sketching
Signed with the artist's monogram, bottom centre. Wootton charged Lord Harley £43 for this picture in 1715; the discrepancy in price with the Newmarket scene above is a reflection of the wealth of portrait-like figures, including the artist's own. Warren Hill is still the training-ground for racehorses based at Newmarket.

Sir GODFREY KNELLER (1646/9–1723)
Bishop Burnet (1643–1715)
Signed lower right: *G Kneller f./1693.*
This is the one picture to have remained at Wimpole since the time of the Hardwickes, and was probably acquired by the 2nd Earl because of his great admiration for the sitter – who was, by contrast, anathema to the Harleys. Gilbert Burnet played a prominent role in the Glorious Revolution of 1688, and was appointed Bishop of Salisbury in 1689. He thus became *ex officio* Chancellor of the Order of the Garter, in whose robes he is shown. The superb Palladian frame may have been carved by Matthias Lock (fl.1710–65).

(?) JAN WEENIX (c.1642–1719)
Still life with poultry and an urn
Weenix's reputation was built on large baroque still-lifes such as this rather than on infrequent portraits such as that in the Entrance Hall. From the Cook Collection, Doughty House, Richmond; bought by Mrs Bambridge in 1959.

Manner of JEAN-BAPTISTE MONNOYER
(1635/6–99)
Still-life with flowers and an urn
Monnoyer was brought over to England around 1690 by Lord Montagu, and painted floral over-doors and overmantels for him and many other noblemen, acquiring the English sobriquet of 'Old Baptist'. He was much imitated. Bought by Mrs Bambridge in 1960.

SCULPTURE

Bronzed plaster busts of Milton and Dryden, by P. Sarti.
Marble bust of a Roman emperor.
Four nineteenth-century French bronzes of *putti*, one pair after Clodion, the other pair by Druot.

THE LORD CHANCELLOR'S ROOM

DECORATION

Grey-veined marble chimney-piece, doorcases and panelled dado, c.1742–5.
Gilt papier-mâché border to the wallpaper, mid-nineteenth century.

STATE BED

The main state bed which probably once stood in a bedchamber to the west of the Saloon was moved up to this room in 1781. Its hangings incorporated

*The Lord
Chancellor's Room*

embroidery of the royal purse given to the 1st Earl of Hardwicke when appointed Lord Chancellor. Although the bed was sold in the 1930s, Mrs Bambridge was able to acquire the present *lit à la polonaise*, a secondary state bed originally from Wimpole. The central canopy and carved Prince of Wales's feathers are *c*.1780; the posts, much of the remaining woodwork, painted white and gold, and the netted hangings date from 1852. A piece of paper inscribed with this date was found when the hangings were restored at the Blickling Textile Conservation Workroom.

PICTURES

Coaching pictures were Capt. Bambridge's first love: a large number from his collection are hung in the first-floor rooms. There are also some charming late eighteenth-century fashion plates and engravings of the gardens at Chiswick. Only original paintings, drawings, pastels and watercolours are noted separately.

OVER THE CHIMNEY-PIECE

ENGLISH, *c*.1850
A Marionette Show
The market square has not yet been identified. Bought by Capt. Bambridge in 1941 for £21.

SPANISH COLONIAL, *c*.1750
Encounter of Spanish and Portuguese commissioners
Watercolour with bodycolour.
Inscribed beneath: *1ᵃ Entre Vista de los Comisarios Espanoles y Portugueses*
Prospectors for precious stones and metals pushing to the frontiers of Brazil led to the need for fresh demarcations of the boundary with the Spanish Viceroyalties in 1750 and 1777. The costumes point to the earlier date; the initials of the negotiators are placed beneath each of them.

FURNITURE

Hepplewhite mahogany wardrobe.
Burr-elm sofa-table, Regency.
Mahogany toilet mirror with brass inlay, Regency.
George III mahogany bedside commode.
One of a set of painted beechwood shield-back chairs, decorated with Prince of Wales's feathers, late eighteenth century.

CERAMICS

Dresden snake-handled vase (lamp), *c*.1860.
Pair of Turkish figures, *c*.1845.

Pairs of nineteenth-century Paris porcelain, Coalport and Spode vases.

CLOCK

Eight-day striking mantel clock in ormolu case, French, *c*.1830. It would originally have stood under a glass dome.

TEXTILES

Embroidered cloth from the Basque region illustrating the five senses, probably late eighteenth century.
Three Tekke rugs from central Asia, early twentieth century. That at the foot of the bed is an *ensi* or door rug, Afghan Kizil Ayak, *c*.1880.

THE LORD CHANCELLOR'S DRESSING ROOM

In 1800 Soane formed this room, and the skylit central Lobby and Study beyond, by subdividing the long gallery which ran across the centre of the house from north to south, and which may have been a feature of the original building. Soane presumably made these changes to compensate for the loss of first-floor rooms when the two-storey Yellow Drawing Room was created. Both Dressing Room and Study were originally planned as bedchambers. Their faceted inner walls reflect the shape of the bay window that Flitcroft added to the north façade in 1745.

PICTURES

(Clockwise, from the left of the entrance door.)

ENGLISH, *c*.1845
The London–Leeds mail coach
Queen Victoria's cipher is on the coach; the signpost shows that it has just come from York. Mail coaches were the fastest – but also the most expensive – form of public transport before they were superseded by trains.

By, and in the manner of, CONSTANTIN GUYS (1802–92)
11 drawings of carriages and figures
Pen and ink, and wash.
Guys, the draughtsman lauded by Baudelaire as 'The Painter [sic] of Modern Life', was in London around 1842 – hence perhaps the English flavour of

some of these drawings. A number, particularly of those in blue ink, appear to be fakes.

ENGLISH, c.1825
At the shoemaker's
Pattison's shoe-shop is reputed to have been at 129 Oxford Street. The younger lady's muslin frock with coloured ribbon belt and voluminous mantle were the height of fashion in the mid-1820s. Bought by Capt. Bambridge in 1941.

J. CORDREY (c.1765–1825)
The London–Liverpool coach
Inscribed on the back of the canvas: *J. CORDREY.*

ENGLISH, c.1840
The Duke of Cambridge and party in their boxes at the Opera
Coloured chalks and wash.
Adolphus Frederick, 1st Duke of Cambridge (1773–1850) was the seventh son of George III, a Field-Marshal, and Viceroy of Hanover from 1816 to 1837. He was a great supporter of charities and the arts, himself a musician, and his popularity was 'emphatically the connecting link between the throne and the people'.

ON THE TABLE

BERNARD-ÉDOUARD SWEBACH (1800–70)
Couple alighting from an open carriage and pair
Panel.
Signed bottom right: *E Swebach.*
Bernard-Édouard was the son of the more famous Metz-born painter François-Joseph Swebach (1769–1823), who called himself Fontaine, or Desfontaines, to make it clear he was not German. He followed his father to Russia (1815–21), collaborated with him, and imitated his subject-matter, mostly in the form of lithographs.

CHARLES THÉVENIN (1764–1838)
The cotton mill, house, and wharf of Richard-Lenoir
Signed bottom right: *C. Thévenin 1809*; inscribed bottom lower right: *Construit/par/Normand A".̲/1809.*
An unusual record of the complex built by the Italianate Neo-classical architect Charles-Pierre-Joseph Normand (1765–1840) for the mill-owner, François Richard, known as Richard-Lenoir (1765–1839), at Chantilly. The house was soon demolished, in 1823; the mill was dismantled by the duc d'Aumale some time after 1830; and only the arched gateway survives. Thévenin may have been the son of the building contractor to Louis XVI, Jacques-Jean Thévenin, which would help to account for

this unusual instance of collaboration between painter and architect. Bought by Capt. Bambridge in May 1941.

FURNITURE
Pair of mahogany sabre-leg chairs, Regency.
Sheraton mahogany sofa-table.
Oval gilt wall-mirror, mid-eighteenth century.
Continental walnut side-table with serpentine front and brass inlays.
Four-drawer mahogany commode, French late nineteenth century.

CERAMICS
Pair of Staffordshire equestrian highwaymen, Dick Turpin and T. King, c.1860.
Group of Staffordshire figures, including collection of lions, and a pair of female figures, one holding a cornucopia, the other a bird.
Flight, Barr and Barr Worcester vase.

CLOCK
Eight-day mantel clock in brass and mahogany case, c.1830.

TEXTILES
Saryk Turkoman or Ersari *ensi* or door rug, early twentieth century.

THE LOBBY

Two pedimented doorcases by Flitcroft; the door on the west wall is now false, for the dome of the Yellow Drawing Room lies beyond.

PICTURES
UNKNOWN, 19th century
Four Flower-pieces
Ovals.
Bought by Mrs Bambridge in 1949.

UNKNOWN, 19th century
Flower-piece
Oval.

FURNITURE
Pair of Continental, carved and gessoed console tables with marble tops.
Inlaid walnut fall-front cabinet, Italian.
Miniature inlaid walnut cabinet with ten drawers and cupboard, Italian.

'A collector in his study', by Wenzel Wehrlin, 1768 (Mrs Bambridge's Study)

CERAMICS AND ENAMELWARE

Strasbourg faience tureen with a lemon on top, by Paul Hannong, *c.*1770.

Meissen tureen with a sliced lemon on top, *c.*1755.

Two Canton enamel dishes with covers, Quian Long (1736–95).

CLOCK

Eight-day striking wall clock in black and gilt painted wooden case, Maltese *c.*1820, with a French movement *c.*1890.

MRS BAMBRIDGE'S STUDY

Created by Soane at the southern end of the former long gallery. Used by Mrs Bambridge as a writing-room, it commands a magnificent view down the south avenue.

PICTURES

(Clockwise, beginning on the left wall as you enter.)

ENGLISH, *c.*1820
An unidentified actor in the role of a coachman
Watercolour.
Effaced inscription beneath.

CHARLES-LOUIS-FRANÇOIS QUINART
(1788–1848) and
HIPPOLYTE LECOMTE (1781–1857)
The duc de Berry shooting an eagle in the Forest of Fontainebleau
Signed bottom mid-left: *Quinart 1818.*
Exhibited in the Salon of 1819, and included in the duchesse de Berry's celebrated collection of contemporary French art. Lecomte painted the figure of the duc de Berry (who was to be assassinated in 1820), and the eagle itself – victim of a lucky shot – was preserved at Bagatelle, Paris, according to the text accompanying the lithograph after this painting. Bought by Capt. Bambridge *c.*1938.

ENGLISH, *c.*1820
An actor in the role of a hussar
Watercolour.
Pendant to the coachman above.

WENZEL WEHRLIN, alias VINCESLAO VERLIN
(1740–80)
A collector in his study
Panel.
Signed under harpsichord: *Wincesl. Wehrlin F./1768.*
The collector sits amongst the impedimenta of his artistic and scientific interests, whilst a putto blowing bubbles, and a number of other objects em-

blematic of human vanity, sit on the floor. Engravings after Watteau's *Embarquement pour Cythère* and *La Mariée de village* on the wall behind him suggest a choice between the distractions of love and an honest marriage.

JACQUES-JOSEPH ('JAMES') TISSOT (1836–1902)
Monochrome study of a seated woman
Panel.
Signed bottom centre: *JT*.
A grisaille study for the first of a pair of scenes of travel, *By Water* and *By Land*, which Tissot exhibited at the Dudley Gallery in 1882. The model is the frequent subject of Tissot's pictures, Kathleen Kelly, Mrs Newton, who became his mistress in 1876, and lived with him until her death from TB in 1882. Bought by Capt. Bambridge in 1937.

WILLIAM FREDERICK WITHERINGTON, RA
(1785–1865)
A Modern Picture Gallery
Signed on stretcher of picture at left:
W. F. Witherington. 1824.
The setting is purely imaginary, including paintings from several different collections. Some half of the thirty-odd visible have so far been identified, ranging from Fuseli's *Saturn surprised by Ithuriel* (far left) and Lawrence's *Kemble as Hamlet* (over door), to Reynolds's *Infant Academy* and Wilson's *View on the Arno* (both to the left of the door). Apparently inspired by Panini's views of equally imaginary galleries, the composition carries the message that contemporary British painting could make every bit as fine a show in a picture gallery as Old Masters, and deserved support. Exhibited RA, 1824, and British Institution, 1825. Bought by Capt. Bambridge in 1941.

GEORGE ELGAR HICKS (1824–1914)
Dividend day at the Bank of England
Board.
Signed bottom right: *GEHicks 1859.*
A sketch for the finished painting (exh. RA 1859; Bank of England), which was one of the pictures with which Hicks made his reputation. Dividend day was the quarterly day when dividends on Bank Stock and Government Securities (known as 'Consols') were paid to personal callers. These were regarded as the safest form of investment – hence the widows shown on the right. The banking hall was designed by Soane, the architect of the Yellow Drawing Room, and embodied a similar use of space.

JAMES TISSOT (1836–1902)
The crack shot
Signed bottom left: *J. J. Tissot 69.*
One of the first pictures Tissot painted in England, it probably shows the garden of Cleeve Lodge, the Hyde Park home of Thomas Gibson Bowles, the editor of *Vanity Fair*. Bowles had invited Tissot over to England to paint the magazine's chief backer, *Col. Burnaby* (1869–70; National Portrait Gallery); the bearded figure in the background may be a portrait of Bowles. Bought by Capt. Bambridge in 1937.

JAMES LYNCH (b.1965)
Bonnie, A Longhorn Cow
Gouache.
Inscribed: *J. Lynch 89.*
Bonnie was bred at Wimpole and was Breed Champion at the Royal Show in 1989. In the background is the Gothic Ruin designed by Sanderson Miller. Commissioned by the Foundation for Art with sponsorship from Oscar & Peter Johnson Ltd.

FURNITURE

The room is furnished with a mixture of English and continental nineteenth- and early twentieth-century pieces, including a mahogany filing cabinet with six drawers, two cupboards below, and ormolu mounts.

CERAMICS AND BRONZES

A collection of nineteenth-century English and continental porcelain, including Staffordshire busts of Harley's friend, Matthew Prior, who died at Wimpole, Handel, Britannia and Neptune.
Five English porcelain vases, gold ground encrusted with flowers, *c.*1820.

ON THE DESK
Four bronze busts: Voltaire and Rousseau at the back; the Duke of Sussex and Duke of York at the front.

CLOCK

Eight-day mantel clock in green painted case, *c.*1820.

TEXTILES

Persian Kashghai carpet, nineteenth century.

MRS BAMBRIDGE'S BEDROOM

FIREPLACE

Grey and white marble chimney-piece. Overmantel designed by Flitcroft and presumably carved by Sefferin Alken between 1742 and 1745.

PICTURES

(Clockwise, beginning to the left of the entrance door.)

JEAN-BAPTISTE-CHARLES CLAUDOT (1733–1805)
Figures before ruins with the statue of Hercules
The first of two large decorative paintings in the manner of the Italian-trained Dijonnais artist, Jean-Baptiste Lallemand (1716–1803), by the eclectic Charles Claudot, who decorated numerous houses in Nancy and elsewhere in Lorraine with similar canvases.

(?) ENGLISH, *c.*1830
Elegant couple paying a call in a carriage and pair
Pen, ink and watercolour.
Despite bearing a French customs stamp on the back (probably attached on Capt. Bambridge's return from France), this would appear to be an English watercolour, by an imitator of Bonington.

PIERRE GAVARNI (1846–after 1883)
A lady on a skewbald horse
Pen, ink and watercolour.
Signed bottom right: *Pierre Gavarni 1872.*
French customs stamps suggest that Capt. Bambridge imported this and the two drawings of *c.*1840, from France.

(?) FRENCH, *c.*1810
An open carriage and four, and other horsemen
Watercolour.

FRENCH, *c.*1840
Two children with their governess offering leaves to the goats of an Italian goat-boy
Watercolour with body colour.

FRENCH, *c.*1840
Two girls reading a letter
Pencil and coloured wash heightened with white.
On the backing: *'Faut-il deux 'R' à M. le Baron?'*
'C'est un homme très vaniteux! . . . Mets-lui en trois, ça le flattera!'. The dialogue is in the manner of that devised by Gavarni for his drawings, but the style is much gentler.

'Windswept girl in a turban walking with a dog', attributed to A. W. Devis (Mrs Bambridge's Bedroom)

Attributed to ARTHUR WILLIAM DEVIS (1762–1822)
Windswept girl in a turban walking with a dog
The slightly exotic buildings, combined with the fantastic turban, suggest that this portrait may have been painted in India. A. W. Devis, son and pupil of Arthur Devis, practised in India in 1785–95, and this picture has much in common with his portraits of children. Bought by Capt. Bambridge in 1942.

JEAN-BAPTISTE-CHARLES CLAUDOT (1733–1805)
Antique ruins with figures and a pyramid
?Dated on a tablet on the pyramid: *177(?)*
Pendant to the above, but apparently coarser in execution. Claudot sometimes worked under severe financial pressure, with adverse results.

(?) FRENCH, early 18th century
Pair of cartouches containing landscapes
Watercolour and gouache.
The inset landscapes are in the manner of Pierre-Antoine Patel the younger (1648–1707).

AUSTRIAN, *c.*1745
The future Emperor Joseph II as a child, in a floral setting
Inscribed on a scroll: JOSEPHUS ARCHIDUX
AUSTRIAE.
The depiction of Archduke Joseph (1741–90) derives from a painting by Martin Mytens of him and three of his sisters in the Schwarzenberg Palace in Vienna, painted in 1744. He is holding up the Order of the Golden Fleece. Bought by Capt. Bambridge in 1941.

FURNITURE

Pair of Provençal walnut chairs with cane backs, Louis XV.
French kingwood *bureau plat* with ormolu mounts.
Continental kingwood 'Semainier', having a drawer for each day of the week, Louis XVI.
Kingwood bedside cupboard, faced with false books.
Central kingwood circular table, possibly Dutch, late eighteenth century.
Pair of continental walnut chests of drawers with parquetry panels and ormolu handles.
Mrs Bambridge's walnut bed is made up with her bed coverings.
Kingwood centre-table with ormolu mounts and floral inlay.

CERAMICS

Pair of reclining Staffordshire figures of Antony and Cleopatra, early eighteenth century.
Coalbrookdale two-handled vase encrusted with flowers.
Pair of porcelain candlesticks by Edmé Saumon (lamps).
Meissen two-handled vase decorated with birds and flowers (lamp).

CENTRE OF ROOM
Oval soft-paste jardinière, probably St Cloud, *c.*1735, in the Meissen style.
French faience two-handled vase after Moustier's original, nineteenth century.
Capodimonte soft-paste porcelain jardinière, *c.*1750.
Circular Staffordshire relief of the Italian patriot, Garibaldi, and two pairs of seated Dalmatian dogs, also Staffordshire.

CLOCKS

Fourteen-day striking clock with Paris porcelain and ormolu case by Rouvière, *c.*1790. The porcelain

obelisks are decorated with figures representing the four continents.
Eight-day 'sedan chair' clock in mahogany case, *c.*1820.

CARPET

Aubusson, nineteenth century.

THE PRINT ROOM

Mrs Bambridge used this as a bathroom. The National Trust redecorated the room in the 1970s and hung the walls with the drawings and engravings which Captain and Mrs Bambridge collected. Engravings of carriages predominate, but there are also costume prints and Gillray cartoons.

FIREPLACE

Miniature chimney-piece and cast-iron grate installed by Soane.

FURNITURE

Six mahogany dining armchairs, continental, early nineteenth century.
Chinese lacquered cabinet on carved and gilded stand, eighteenth century.
Painted corner cupboard, eighteenth century.

CERAMICS

Yellow ground jardinières, Faubourg St Denis, Paris, *c.*1790.

THE SERVANTS' STAIRCASE

Added by Soane against the east wall of the seventeenth-century house; the top of Flitcroft's blocked window, which formerly lit the main staircase on the other side of the wall, is clearly visible.

THE BATH HOUSE

It was designed by Soane for the 3rd Earl of Hardwicke around 1792, and placed in what had been an open courtyard to the east of the original seventeenth-century house, and between Gibbs's chapel and Kenton Couse's Great Dining Room. Entered on a mezzanine level via an Ante-Chamber, with an open fire for warming and drying. The plunge bath, heated at one time by a boiler in the basement, holds some 2,199 gallons of water, and was presumably fed from the *Castello d'Aqua*, a contemporary reservoir building constructed by Soane in the park and long since demolished. By the mid-eighteenth century bath houses were a not uncommon appendage to the English country house (see Chapter Four). They were, however, usually placed in the park, and were considered old-fashioned by the time Soane built the one at Wimpole. The Bath House was restored in 1980 after damage from dry rot. Beside the bath stands an early nineteenth-century shower, made by Alexander Boyd of New Bond Street.

DECORATION

The present scheme reproduces Soane's decoration. The walls are lined out to look like stone masonry,

The Bath House

while the stone shelf around the bath is painted to simulate boarding. The Ante-Chamber walls are stippled to resemble granite and all the woodwork is grained, the softwood handrails in imitation of mahogany.

THE CHAPEL

This great Baroque interior was created in the 1720s for Lord Harley, despite the fact that the parish church lay only a few yards away. It may have been conceived in conscious rivalry of the Duke of Chandos's famous chapel at Canons, and as a suitable setting for performances by Harley's orchestra, although a marginal note on the score of an anthem composed by Dr Tudway, Harley's music master, records that it was never consecrated. The Chapel was designed by Gibbs, whose earliest drawings date from 1713, and decorated by Sir James Thornhill. The original intention seems to have been to form an arcaded and vaulted interior in stone and plaster. In the event the architecture above the panelling is entirely painted in *trompe l'oeil*.

DECORATION

The scheme comprises an arcade of coupled Corinthian columns supporting a hexagonal coffered ceiling. On the north wall niches house four gilded 'statues' of the four Doctors of the Church – Gregory, Ambrose, Augustine and Jerome – a near repetition of Thornhill's decoration of the chapel at All Souls College, Oxford. (Curiously and perhaps no more than coincidentally in this context, the east wall of Thornhill's All Souls scheme featured the *Resurrection of Archbishop Chichele*, who had owned Wimpole in the fifteenth century.)

The east wall, representing the *Adoration of the Magi*, which Thornhill executed on canvas, has been described with justice as 'the most notable Baroque rendering of a religious subject by an English painter'. The arrangement is thought to have been inspired by Inigo Jones's Queen's Chapel at St James's with its great Venetian east window. The delicate blues and pinks in the Virgin's dress may reflect the influence of the Venetian painters, Sebastiano Ricci and his rival, Giovanni Antonio Pellegrini, but Thornhill may also have been studying the more classical work of Poussin and other late seventeenth-century French artists. Ricci and Pellegrini were popular with many English patrons in the early eighteenth century, although not Harley, who thought Pellegrini's murals at Narford Hall in Norfolk 'done by very bad hands'. The more characteristic muted orange browns and maroons of the three kings' robes would probably have been preferred by Harley.

On the west wall, above the family pew, are three *trompe l'oeil* vases with 'bas reliefs' of the Baptism of Christ, the Last Supper and the Resurrection. Thornhill received £1,350 for the work, which he completed in 1724; his signature and the date are painted on the lintel to the glazed door leading into the Entrance Hall. Thornhill's illusionistic style and predominantly sombre colouring were not particularly fashionable by this time, and Harley may have commissioned the work to help his friend's career. Whatever Harley's reasons, Thornhill's decoration of the Chapel shows him at the height of his powers and must be considered among his finest religious work.

Drawers and bins in the Dry Store

FURNISHINGS

The oak panelling and the hexagonal pulpit, with its inlaid panels, are original, but box pews for the servants are shown in the body of the chapel in Flitcroft's survey of 1742. These must have been converted at some later stage into two rows of stalls facing each other. Payments to the blacksmith Thomas Warren, best known for his wrought-iron gates at Clare College, Cambridge, occur among Harley's account books alongside those to Thornhill, and he must therefore have been responsible for the splendid ironwork of the communion rail. The gilt altar table, carved with winged cherubs, is similar to that in the Church and was probably designed by Flitcroft – together with the carved frame above it. Jeremiah Milles recorded in 1735 seeing a reredos by Thornhill here, representing 'our Saviour and Nicodemus'. The torchères came from Lanhydrock.

THE HOUSEKEEPER'S ROOM AND DRY STORE

This is the first of a series of basement rooms that will be gradually added to the visitor route. From here the Housekeeper would have managed the affairs of the household for her mistress; her authority was second only to the Steward's. She was responsible for the household furniture, linen and all the grocery. The Dry Store is only accessible from the Housekeeper's Room. The Housekeeper's furniture was presumably disposed of in the sales of the 1930s, and it seems likely that Mrs Bambridge introduced the present large cupboards when she demolished Kendall's east service wing in 1952. They were clearly not designed for the room – the cornice of each has been crudely cut to accommodate the central ceiling beam. The cupboard and drawer handles are identical to those on the mid-nineteenth-century Dry Store furniture. The glazed cupboard now houses part of the Robert Hirsch collection of ceramic strainers. Display material describes the changing layout of the service quarters and the role of the servants.

THE BASEMENT CORRIDOR

The corridor leads back past the lobby outside the Chapel and into the east corridor. The Dairy, Pantry, Brushing Room, Shoe Room and Knife Room are to the left, the Lamp Room on the right. The glazed door at the end of the corridor formerly led up to the Kitchen, storerooms, larders, Bakehouse and Brewery housed within Kendall's east service wing. Another passage leads back, on the ground floor, to two tea-rooms.

THE DINING ROOM

Remodelled by Kendall in the 1840s on the site of a smaller, apsidal-ended 'Eating Room' designed by Flitcroft's assistant Kenton Couse in 1778. Couse's design showing the ceiling plasterwork with the walls 'folded' down around it, may be seen in the Red Room. Kendall extended the room to the east by one bay.

DECORATION

In 1949 Kendall's doorcases, dado panelling, marble fireplace and overmantel were stripped out by the Bambridges, whose architect Trenwith Wills divided the room up to make pantries and a kitchen; this idea may have been suggested to them by the 1935 plans commissioned by Philip Yorke, which show a very similar subdivision of the room. In the 1970s the National Trust removed the partitions and false ceiling, to expose Kendall's gilded plasterwork above. The plasterwork incorporates the monogram CR and a viscount's coronet, in celebration of the birth of the 4th Earl's son and heir, Charles, Viscount Royston. The chimney-piece in carved wood and plaster with glazed panels, displaying gilded flowers by Claud Yorke of the 1930s, was given by David Yorke and installed in 1990.

PICTURES

Studio of FRANZ XAVER WINTERHALTER
(1805–73)
Queen Victoria
The original, for which the Queen sat in 1842, is in the Royal Collection, along with a pendant of Prince Albert; she considered the likeness 'perfect'. This is one of innumerable copies from Winterhalter's studio, probably painted for the 4th Earl when Lord-in-Waiting to the Queen (1841–7). Kindly lent by the present Earl of Hardwicke.

JOHN WOOTTON (*c.*1682–1764)
The Countess of Oxford's Dun Mare, held by Thomas Thornton the Groom
John Wootton wrote about this picture to Lord Harley's steward, William Ovington, on 16 May 1715: 'Be pleas'd to let my Lord know yᵉ great Picture of yᵉ Dunn Mare is finnish'd, nothing is wanting to compleat it but Thomas's sweet Face; that Picture comes to forty guineas . . .'. The Dun Mare is the same as in the smaller picture in the Entrance Hall, but everything else is different. The English fashion for life-size portraits of horses began

in the mid-seventeenth century with the dozen of the 1st Duke of Newcastle's *manège* horses ascribed to Diepenbeke, but possibly actually by Jacob Pieter Gowi (fl.1632–61), which are still at Welbeck Abbey.

JENNENS & BETTRIDGE of Birmingham, *c.*1845
Four views of palaces
Mechanical paintings on papier mâché.
Senate Square, St Petersburg, with Falconet's statue of Peter the Great
Edward Blore's Mall façade of Buckingham Palace
Windsor Castle
Peterhof
Jennens & Bettridge took over the Birmingham papier mâché factory of Henry Clay, the inventor of 'paper ware', in 1816, and flourished until 1864. One of their employees, G. Neville, discovered a technique of painting on black papier mâché in 1831, but left them in 1846. The effect here is not particularly successful, merely looking like inferior oils on canvas.

THE BREAKFAST ROOM

Used by Mrs Bambridge as a writing-room and subsequently as a dining-room. A survey plan of 1940 describes it as the School Room. Marble chimney-piece of the Flitcroft period, with a wooden overmantel probably carved by Alken. The baron's coronet in the fireplace frieze dates it before 1754, the year he became an earl. Plasterwork ceiling, with busts of four Emperors in medallions by Kendall *c.*1842. The walls are hung with facsimiles of watercolours of Kendall's demolished conservatory wing. The original watercolours are possibly the work of Thomas Allom, a draughtsman and perspectivist often employed by Kendall.

CHAPTER NINE
THE GARDENS AND PARK

Humphry Repton had a telling phrase for every situation whenever he was called upon to formulate a garden design. Wimpole was no exception. In the Red Book he compiled for the 3rd Earl of Hardwicke in 1801 he wrote:

The counties of Cambridge and Huntingdon consist generally of flat ground and cornfields with few hedges or trees; while the few hills are yet more naked; but Wimpole abounds in beautiful shapes of ground and is richly clothed with wood – it is therefore like a flower in the desert, beautiful in itself but more beautiful by its situation.[1]

With allowance for a justifiable measure of hyperbole, that description still appears a fair one. Wimpole lies right on the junction between the flat clay lands of west Cambridgeshire and the rising chalk ground that extends eventually to form the Chilterns. The successive owners of Wimpole since the Chicheleys have exploited this topographical variety in making their parks and gardens. The views in each direction are quite different. To the south, the land opens up with wide vistas, while to the north and east the land rises into rolling, wooded hills. Beyond the small formal garden around the house, there is now mainly open parkland dotted with trees, with farmland and woodland beyond; as in many great park landscapes, this is the result of generations of expansion and management.

The parkland's earliest landscape features are medieval. The first reference to a park at Wimpole occurs at the very beginning of the fourteenth century, around the principal manor house. By the time the map of the estate was drawn by Benjamin Hare in 1638, there were two deer parks to the west of the old house, the High and Low Parks, marked by banks which still survive. (They probably

Watercolour from Repton's Red Book, showing his suggested improvements to the Wimpole lake

incorporate the headlands from the earlier field system where the ploughs would turn.) An avenue of walnut trees divided the two, while a wood called Rook Grove filled the area to the north-east of the house. Beyond were the fields and settlements that made up the parish.

When Sir Thomas Chicheley replaced the old house with his new mansion after 1640, he extended the formal style of the house out into the landscape, constructing a rectangular formal garden around the Hall on the same north–south basis, and cutting into the old woods. The fields and the hamlet to the south and south-west of the house were taken into the parkland, with the inhabitants relocated in new farmsteads, and a grand new avenue some 90 feet wide was planted south from the Hall to the roadway. These elm and chestnut trees may have been an early example of planting on the 'quincunx' plan, with each group of five trees planted on the corners and centre of a square: they then presented parallel alleys when viewed from different angles. Chicheley's garden provided the bones for the considerably grander schemes on which the 2nd Earl of Radnor spent so much of his fortune after he acquired Wimpole in 1683, with 'all the most exquisite contrivances which the best heads could invent to make it artificially as well as naturally pleasant', as Daniel Defoe put it.[2] There was a strong French and Dutch influence in the formal enclosed garden, extended to the north of the house, with its parterres and fountains, intersecting hedged alleys and wrought-iron gates, and 'the best heads' were probably those on the shoulders of the Royal gardeners George London and Henry Wise, while William Talman and the Royal smith and designer Jean Tijou may have contributed a new orangery and gates. Kip's engraved view suggests that further avenues were planted and a larger area emparked. Water played a prominent part in the extravagant new designs: a water garden was constructed to the south-west of the house, and a chain of ponds to the south-east, while large fish ponds with plantations of trees behind were added away to the north. Johnson's Hill, the high point exactly to the north of the house, was incorporated into the garden design by the addition of a large avenue that led directly towards it.

Three horse chestnuts are the survivors of Radnor's planting schemes which were to set the framework for all the garden works which followed. Between about 1720 and 1725 Charles Bridgeman, one of those high in the favour of Edward, Lord Harley, added still more avenues in the parkland and radically simplifed Radnor's north garden. He extended the ancient lime avenue on the southern boundary to join Radnor's Scots pine avenue in the old park. He planted a grid of limes and horse chestnuts west of the house, and a new avenue leading north-west from the house, so incorporating the medieval mill mound from the ancient field system into the park. The church spire at Whaddon away to the south-west became a garden feature, as Bridgeman cut through one of Radnor's avenues to provide a vista.

The most dramatic gesture ever made in the Wimpole park was Bridgeman's enormous South Avenue, running for over two miles in parallel lines of elm trees 50 feet apart across a central space of 90 yards. The avenue ran down across the Cambridge road, swept round an octagonal basin, and continued until it reached the Great North Road. Aerial photographs taken in the 1940s show the mature grandeur of Bridgeman's avenue, which had been allowed to remain despite all the subsequent changes in gardening fashion, cutting a swathe through a patchwork of fields and hedgerows, the stuff of the ordinary countryside. The depredations of Dutch elm disease in the 1970s, which led to the felling of the avenue and its replanting with limes grafted from mother trees in the park, and the grubbing up of many hedgerows by farmers in this part of the county, now make these aerial photographs just as valuable historical documents as the garden plans of the master garden designers themselves.

Successive generations of those gardeners stripped away this formality, although all left the South Avenue intact. Robert Greening was the first professional gardener to be employed by the Earls of Hardwicke, with guidance provided by the manuscript notes of 'Mr S' (who may have been the poet William Shenstone) and his friend Sanderson Miller. In the early 1750s the formality of the north garden was softened with the removal of the parterres and formal plantings, and the laying of a

The South Avenue from the air in 1949. This photograph also shows Kendall's Victorian wings and towers, demolished in 1953

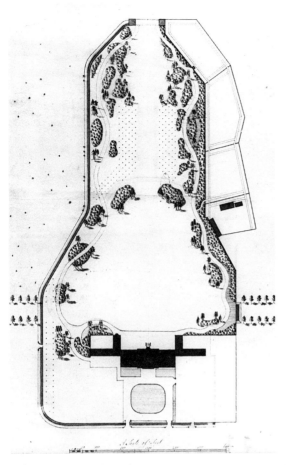

Robert Greening's design for replanting the garden north of the house in a more informal style, c.1752

lawn with serpentine walks between the trees planted around the edges. Views to the west were opened up by cutting through Bridgeman's grid of trees, while considerable extensions of parkland were made for the first time to the east. At the same time fences and gates were comprehensively replaced with ha-has. One of Greening's specialities was in fruit and walled gardens, and he provided detailed planting instructions for the kitchen garden to the north-east, complete with 'a hot wall' heated by flues from a fire, against which exotic fruit could be grown – Brussels and Orange apricots, Duke cherries, Temple nectarines and greengages.

From the mid-1760s until the mid-1770s, the most famous name in English gardening history,

Lancelot 'Capability' Brown, worked at Wimpole. Brown continued the process of destruction of many of the formal features, felling the north and north-west avenues and most of the western double lime avenue, although individual trees were left as the basis for his characteristic clumps. More farmland was incorporated into the park: a map survives in the house showing the old field boundaries and hedges with occupiers' names, and then the smooth grassland of the same area after Brown had had his way. To the north, Radnor's fish-ponds became the first in a series of artificial lakes at the foot of Johnson's Hill, with islands created in them, and crossed by a 'Chinese' bridge. The present bridge, which has been restored by the National Trust, is probably a Victorian replica of Brown's bridge incorporating the same decorative detail of curved rails and round wooden balls.

The Gothic Tower was built on Johnson's Hill in 1774, to the reworked designs of James Essex based on that which Sanderson Miller had proposed to the 1st Earl twenty-five years before as an early example of the Georgian Gothic revival. It consists of three part-ruined circular towers connected by curtain walls, all built in clunch (the local chalky stone), brick and rubble. Bogus medieval inscriptions added to the mystery of what became the most eye-catching element of the Wimpole landscape. The 2nd Earl of Hardwicke's final addition to his park was 'Athenian' Stuart's Prospect House on the western rise (now gone).

After a gap of some fifteen years, the new 3rd Earl introduced Brown's former pupil William Emes to the estate. The final elements of formal gardening disappeared, as Emes dismantled the shrubberies north of the house and filled in the ha-ha and created a new walled garden in its present woodland position further to the north-east, demolishing Bridgeman and Greening's old garden. Meanwhile the park had been extended further still to the south-west, where belts of trees sheltered it from the Great North Road. One element of formality was re-introduced, a short avenue framing the view of the folly tower.

It was this scene – albeit a simpler one than Emes had proposed – which greeted Repton in 1801, and provided him with the occasion for his celebrated outburst against the excesses of informal land-scaping. Repton's proposals included an enclosed garden to the north of the house with a formal garden between the two main wings and a wall and railings around. These were also to make 'a proper use . . . of the vases in the park some of which have kept their ancient stations, although the trees which formerly accompanied them have been removed'. Robert Withers, the Wimpole land agent, probably laid these gardens out, and they are shown in the map he made in 1825. Elsewhere, Repton heightened the informality by extending and thickening Brown's belts of trees on the margins of the park. The other picturesque touches which he proposed seem not to have been implemented.

Most of the Victorian works in the Wimpole landscape seem to have been consolidation rather than the devising of new schemes. Shrubberies were planted in the pleasure grounds to the north and east of the house, and there are good specimens of conifers, including a golden Chinese Juniper in the shrubbery that leads towards the walled garden and Home Farm. Other Victorian features, like the 'Archery Ground', seem not to have survived; in recent years, a simplified version of the Victorian formal parterres in the enclosed north garden between the house's wings has been re-established. New wooded plantations like the Victoria Plantation away to the east and extensions to Cobbs Wood added considerably to the amount of standing timber on the estate, while under the 4th Earl management of the timber interests was placed on a sound commercial footing. The cricket ground laid out to the south of the house, complete with two pavilions, one for the village and one for the family from the Hall, was removed at the beginning of the Second World War; unlike the Clifdens, neither Captain nor Mrs Bambridge seem to have been great cricket-lovers. Mrs Bambridge's greatest contribution to the Wimpole garden is to be seen in springtime. Daffodils were her joy, and many were planted and naturalised during her years of ownership, often the most newly introduced varieties, from 'Fortune' and 'Beersheba' of the 1920s to 'Red

The Chinese Bridge

Rascal' and 'Mrs Barclay' of the 1950s. In 1987 a rose garden was laid out on the site of Kendall's conservatory which Mrs Bambridge had demolished. It consists chiefly of old shrub roses including *Rosa rugosa* 'Blanc Double de Coubert', 'Buff Beauty' and Rose 'Nevada' planted among Portugal Laurels and *Viburnum tinus* 'Eve Price'.

The trees were the greatest glory of Wimpole; their relative neglect in the twentieth century has left a landscape which by comparison with its surroundings is heavily wooded, yet is but a shadow of its former magnificence. In spite of the changes which have taken place, a few old trees still survive from the very early schemes at Wimpole. To maintain this unusual continuity with the past considerable work has been carried out in the park and gardens since 1976, and eventually Wimpole will again, in Repton's words, 'be richly clothed with wood'.

THE CHURCH

St Andrew's parish church, together with the rectory and the stables, make a close-knit group alongside the Hall. The church and the former rectory (the latter the property of the National Trust, privately let and not open) have always been an integral part of the estate. No other houses stand nearby, a legacy of the long process of settlement change and extension of the parkland. The church has always been the focus of the parish's life, whether parishioners were dispersed or lived nearby, and despite the occasional lapse. John Docwra in 1510 left half a mark in his will 'to the High Altar for tithes negligently forgotten', and the curate was displaced after the Civil War, as 'a man very negligent in the ministerial office, and much given to play at cards of a night.'

The main structure of Wimpole church dates from 1749. In April 1748 a somewhat larger medieval church, shown on Kip's bird's-eye view, was completely demolished with the exception of the fourteenth-century Chicheley chapel, and then rebuilt to the designs of Henry Flitcroft. What Flitcroft built for Lord Chancellor Hardwicke was essentially an aisleless brick box, with a pedimented west end, stone-faced and topped by a bellcote.

(The bell itself dates from 1653.) Much of the exterior and the interior of the church were Gothicised in the later nineteenth century, with the doorway and the windows on the south side given new pointed forms and tracery. Designs for these survive, signed by George Evans in April 1868, but the exact date the work was undertaken is uncertain. Flitcroft's west gallery was renewed with, in Sir Nikolaus Pevsner's words, 'an elephantiasis of Gothic forms'; the eighteenth-century heraldic stained glass of Yorke family coats of arms in the gallery windows was kept. Underneath the gallery, just inside the entrance door, stands a crisply carved Victorian font together with an engraving of the battered old baptismal font it replaced. The carved wooden reredos at the altar end, another part of Flitcroft's building, which was originally blank except for painted tablets of the Commandments and the Lord's Prayer in the eighteenth-century fashion, was also altered in the nineteenth century, when a stained-glass Venetian window was inserted. The wrought-iron communion rails, which recall those of the chapel, were installed early in this century as a family memorial to the 6th Viscount Clifden.

THE CHICHELEY CHAPEL

The principal impression the church gives is of an assembly of monuments, especially in the north chapel, reached through the large round archway in the nave wall. The chapel was restored in 1732 by Lord Oxford, survived the Flitcroft rebuilding, and was opened to the body of the church during the Victorian remodelling. Previously, the chapel had been walled off and had a separate entrance.

STAINED GLASS

The central window in the chapel's north wall blazes with a variety of re-set, mainly heraldic, fourteenth-century stained glass. The thirteen coats of arms principally record families who held land in and around Wimpole – Bassingbourn, Avenel, Tiptoft – as well as the arms of England and France. They surround the figure of a pilgrim, and the backgrounds and borders are composed of other heraldic fragments.

(Opposite page) The Gothic Tower

THE FAMILY MONUMENTS

Most prominent of the monuments, because it occupies the centre of the Chicheley chapel, is the tomb effigy of the 3rd Earl of Hardwicke, executed by Richard Westmacott the younger in 1844. He lies there asleep, in his Garter robes, his coronet at his feet. This is one of the more recent monuments; the oldest are three sixteenth-century brasses, now set in the walls on either side of the entrance arch. Below the north window stands the tomb of Sir Thomas Chicheley, who died in 1616. His family are represented as mourners around the sides of the chest on which lies his recumbent coloured effigy; the boy represented kneeling on the front of the tomb chest is traditionally supposed to be the Sir Thomas who built the new house at Wimpole.

That he does not have his own monument here is because he sold the estate. No subsequent owner died in possession of Wimpole until Lord Chancellor Hardwicke, who is commemorated in the grandest of all the monuments, by James 'Athenian'

Stuart and Peter Scheemakers, in the centre of the east wall. They also collaborated on the smaller monument to Catherine Yorke, *née* Freman (mother of the 3rd Earl), and Scheemakers alone was responsible for the memorial to her husband, the unfortunate Hon. Charles Yorke who died in 1770 just before his could assume the Lord Chancellorship which had been his life's ambition. The monument nevertheless shows the purse with the royal arms, which is the badge of the Lord Chancellor's office. Among other family monuments in the chapel is the Neo-classical urn with mourning figures by Sir Richard Westmacott the elder, the memorial to the Hon. John Yorke who died in 1801, youngest son of the 1st Earl. More family memorials fill the walls of the chancel and church.

Captain and Mrs Bambridge lie together just outside the west door of the church, their grave marked by a curved headstone that simply records their names, dates and Captain Bambridge's Military Cross.

The Stables, built by Kendall in 1852

THE STABLES

The original stables of the 1690s had stood just to the south of the church: the Stuart building is shown in Kip's engraved view, and Henry Flitcroft's survey plan shows the individual stalls crammed into what was quite a small brick building. This was insufficient for the grandeur of the enlarged Wimpole in the 4th Earl of Hardwicke's day, and H. E. Kendall was commissioned to design a new, larger stable block, to be set further back from the house than its predecessor. Kendall's proposals included a rather chaste plain block with a short central tower, but what Lord Hardwicke finally had erected in 1852 (some ten years after they were designed) were stables in a Victorian version of the late Stuart baroque.

Built of red brick with stone dressings, the stabling was arranged around three sides of a great inner courtyard paved in granite setts. Entry to the stable block is through a grand archway surmounted by a tall clock turret and cupola, flanked by the Hardwicke heraldic stag and lion which were cast in artificial stone (probably by M. H. Blanchard). The skyline is also enlivened by segmental pediments on the end bays of each elevation, and a large number of stone balls on plinths between them. At a later date, cottages were inserted into the four corners of the stable block, some of which only received light from windows looking into the deep cast-iron verandah that runs round the inside of the courtyard.

NOTES

1 The Wimpole Red Book is preserved in the house.

2 D. Defoe, *A tour through the whole island of Great Britain* (1724–6; Penguin edition, Harmondsworth, 1971), p.10.

3 BL, Add MS 39814. fo. 304; Bodleian Library, MS Rawl. D 924, fo. 186.

CHAPTER TEN
THE ESTATE

Wimpole Hall lies at the centre of a substantial landed estate. Mrs Bambridge bequeathed some 2,400 acres to the National Trust in 1976, but at the heyday of the Earls of Hardwicke's ownership the estate covered over 11,000 acres in this part of Cambridgeshire (as well as another 8,000 acres elsewhere, in the Cambridgeshire Fens, and in Hertfordshire, Hampshire and Suffolk). Wimpole and Arrington parishes were almost totally owned by the families at Wimpole Hall from the Chicheleys in the seventeenth century until the Clifdens at the beginning of the twentieth. People worked for the Hall or for the tenants in the farms, and the shops and carriers relied on trade from the great estate.

The nearby Great North Road also brought trade. Recent excavations where the Cambridge road joins it at Arrington Bridge have revealed the Roman equivalent of a motorway service station, a stabling and refreshment complex. There was almost certainly a third-century settlement along the road, with small fields running into the Wimpole estate's eastern side. By the time of Domesday Book in 1086, there were three settlements, Wimpole, Wratworth and Whitwell. (Their total value was £20 8s.) By 1279 the three settlements had been absorbed into one, with six manors within it. The subsequent story through to the seventeenth century is of consolidation of ownership until Sir John Cutler came to own everything in 1686.

Wimpole's open, communally farmed fields still existed into the early seventeenth century, although some enclosure into separate fields and farmsteads had already happened. The medieval strips are still visible in many areas of the park: some of the clearest areas of 'ridge and furrow' are to be seen in the parkland west of the house, enclosed at an early date to form the deer park, and so relatively undisturbed. A mound with a few trees on it, beside the footpath to the Gothic Tower, is the site of the former mill, standing on what was an access track-way where three former fields met. Benjamin Hare's 1638 estate map shows a four-sail wooden post-mill on this spot.

By the later seventeenth century, large-scale enclosure of the former fields had been carried out, eradicating the areas of common land. Until then Wimpole parish had been a multi-centred settlement, possibly reflecting the earlier history of scattered settlement that the Domesday Book recorded. The maps and ground remains indicate the presence of a number of small settlements that were destroyed in the process of emparkment during the seventeenth century. Bennall End lay south-west of the Hall, alongside the road which is now the drive from Arrington gates; Thresham End was just south of the Hall, beyond the point where the chain of ponds was dug in Lord Radnor's day. Only slight earthworks survive there today, but there are some successor buildings to other hamlets: the eighteenth-century cottages at Brick End north of the Home Farm (which Repton had wanted covered with trellis and roses to make a landscape feature) stand where another hamlet had been, and Cobbs Wood Farm to the east has the wooded mound where a moated manor house once stood. The population in this part of Cambridgeshire was falling in the late Tudor and early Stuart periods – in contrast to what was happening in most other areas – so the clearing of these hamlets and establishment of new farms scattered through the estate may have been more an act of common-sense than the hard-hearted arrogance of landscape designers. Thereafter, there were usually some eight to ten tenanted farms in the parish, each of 100 to 200 acres, plus the home farm.

The main farming land is of heavy Cambridgeshire gault clay, suitable for pasture and some cropping. Dr William Stratford wrote to Lord Harley, 'I am far from having any disadvantageous

Watercolour of farm cottages on the Wimpole estate, from Repton's Red Book

opinion of Wimpole. I think it for the summer as delicious a spot as in England . . . [But the clay means it cannot] be wholesome in the winter.'[1] Pasture was usually poor on this inadequately drained land.

We know most about the farming on the estate in the period after 1740. The eighteenth-century cropping patterns appear to have been a rotation of two crops and fallow on arable land and cow pasture. The 1st and 2nd Earls of Hardwicke's stewards would usually keep the estate owners informed of market prices and estate affairs. Alarm spread in 1748 and 1755 about the cattle distempers that were sweeping the country, while the perennial Georgian problem of the poor exercised the minds of the Earls and their correspondents, for example in June 1781, with 'the scantiness of the crops of grain, not affording full employment for the labouring poor.'[2]

The later eighteenth century was a time when some estate owners were beginning to take a greater interest in the cause of agricultural improvement: promoting enclosure of land, encouraging the growing of new crops, building model farms to satisfy their tastes for the architecturally bizarre and their wish to demonstrate good practice. The 2nd Lord Hardwicke felt almost embarrassed that he allowed matters to jog along much as they had always done. For his nephew and heir, when he acquired Wimpole in 1790, it was quite different.

Earlier guidebook writers were struck by the success the 3rd Earl had:

His lordship's farming establishment is on a very extensive scale; and, from every improved method in agriculture being judiciously introduced, the produce of his grounds is yearly increasing. The drill husbandry . . . [and] various other inventions to facilitate the labours of the agriculturalist, are on this establishment attended to in proportion to their utility.[3]

Improvements took many forms. The Home Farm which Soane designed was intended to represent best practice and to act in part as an experimental unit. Improvement of the soil was a priority, especially through deep ploughing and better drainage. Guidance in these matters was given by the agent brought from Scotland, where farming improvements had been popular on great estates for longer.

New crops and products were tried: one year, carrots had been grown very successfully, 'but the number of bushels could not be ascertained, from the depredations of people stealing them'; another year a woman came over from Soham to instruct the dairymaid (probably without success) in the making of the Cambridgeshire soft cheeses. Some of the earliest farm machinery was tried out, most notably a water-driven threshing mill for corn which was installed on Thornberry Hill Farm by 1804 to a Scottish design. (The building, later a corn mill and then a barn, survived until the mid-1970s.) Animal breeding was put on a firmer basis: a Leicester/Lincoln sheep cross was introduced to the estate, in the wake of a massive outbreak of sheep rot. New deer stocks were also introduced, for their predecessors had been almost wiped out in the late 1780s by a mysterious disease which included bursts of mad behaviour.

Lord Hardwicke also tried moral reformation, being caring towards the poor to whom he regularly gave bounties in cash and in kind. Prizes were given for the best-kept and most productive cottage gardens. The Rev. James Plumptre, visiting Wimpole in 1800 to witness this, was suitably impressed,

Workers in the Wimpole timber yard in the late nineteenth century

making 'each of these sons (or rather daughters, for only the women were at home) of industry a present of the *Information for cottagers* which I had brought for that purpose and with which they seemed highly pleased.'[4]

All this was successful in raising the profile and the profitability of the estate. For a short period from 1814 Lord Hardwicke became President of the Board of Agriculture, taking a leading national role in the cause of agricultural improvement in the post-Napoleonic War depression. Success had a price, however. An anonymous correspondent in 1802 wrote that there was a general belief that when their leases expired Lord Hardwicke's tenants would be turned out, or expected to pay hugely increased rents to maintain the pace of change. This, his informant said, made Lord Hardwicke deeply unpopular. Nearly thirty years later, Wimpole was affected by the nationwide explosion of anger and violence among labourers directed against mechanical threshing and other labour-saving devices.

Wimpole's heyday was probably the middle years of the nineteenth century. Prices, especially for grain, were good. Commercial digging for coprolites – phosphatic nodules which were an important early fertiliser – earned Lord Hardwicke great sums in the 1860s. The woodlands were treated as a commercial venture, with the construction of a sizeable woodyard and sawmill and employing dozens of fellers, woodsmen, and carpenters. Brickmaking became another estate activity, while gas for lighting was provided by the estate's own gas works (adjacent to the woodyard). Wimpole had considerable fame as a sporting estate. Large areas were dedicated to the pheasant, and numerous estate workers employed preparing the birds for shoots and deterring poachers. When the estate was offered for sale in 1891, the sale catalogues and newspaper articles laid particular stress on its sporting attributes, and it was on a shooting weekend that George Bambridge was first introduced to Wimpole. Such prosperity and the benevolence of the Yorke family was reflected in the construction from 1849 of new cottages and a school in what became known as New Wimpole, the village that straggles along the Cambridge road to the south of the park.

With the agricultural depression of the 1870s, which affected many arable areas, especially in eastern England, the tide of profitability began to turn. The speed with which 'Champagne Charlie', the 5th Earl, ran through his inheritance compounded the difficulties. Depressed conditions lasted until the Second World War, with pasture and animals rather than crops becoming the mainstay. In common with many country estates, Wimpole slid into low returns and apathy. The progressive sales of outlying farms did contribute to the rise in owner-occuperiship of farms, as tenants were able to buy their property. Even the great Home Farm, built by Soane as a showpiece, had deteriorated sadly by the 1950s and '60s. Agricultural revival in recent years has seen the restoration of farming prosperity in and around Wimpole, and considerably greater emphasis on crop-growing than had been the case for well over a century.

THE HOME FARM

Sir John Soane's model farm is one of the prime survivals of the agricultural improving zeal which seems to have gripped the English and Scottish landowning classes in the late eighteenth century. The farm was built north-east of the main house, but close enough by so that Lord Hardwicke could keep a watchful eye over it.

The model farms were planned to be *integrated* working units as well as architectural conceits. Each element of the design had its place in a complex farming system which Soane, and other late Georgian architects, attempted to express. Buildings, often set in a square or an oval, were ranged around yards where manure might be stored, hay and straw placed in ricks, or animals walked through. The main elements were a barn for storing and threshing grain, cow stalls, stables for the working horses, pigsties, cart sheds, a slaughter area, and at a suitable remove, a dairy. All these elements appeared in Soane's plan for Wimpole of 1792, and most survived to be restored during the 1980s. An octagonal dairy and the farm-house were not to be built until 1860, although a dairy in a picturesque rustic mode had certainly been intended. Soane's detailed drawings even included little Neo-classical hen boxes, but these too were not built, although a series of deer pens (to maintain stocks after the disastrous outbreak of disease among the park deer) was subsequently used as hen houses.

The great thatched barn, with its double entrances opening on to threshing floors, now houses an exhibition of farming life on the estate, organised around the seasons of the year and the tasks associated with them: draining, ploughing, sowing, harvesting, threshing. Some of the tools, such as the Smythe seed drill or the Scotch manure cart, were used at Wimpole in the 3rd Earl's day. The Marshall threshing machine was still in use for oats at the Wimpole Home Farm in the 1950s; it is a direct descendant of the very early machines which the 3rd Earl introduced soon after 1800, superseding the hand flails previously used on the new barn's threshing floors.

When the 3rd Earl died in 1834, the inventory taken at the farm showed what a great range of tools and implements it had. For breaking down the soil, there were 'five pairs of 4-beam harrows, a pair of large harrows, and two sets of gingling harrows', as well as sixteen different ploughs (including a snow plough).[5] The farm had already outgrown the accommodation which Soane had designed – there were fifteen carts and more waggons besides, whereas the cartsheds had been planned for eight carts and two waggons. There were 12 dairy cows, 45 neatstock, 14 cart horses, 697 sheep and 48 other animals in 1834. Later in the nineteenth century cows became more important, so some of Soane's buildings were pulled down and new buildings erected, making it no longer quite the farm he designed and built.

When Mrs Bambridge bequeathed Wimpole to the National Trust in 1976, the Home Farm was barely recognised as the treasure it has proved to be. Extensive restoration has rescued Soane's buildings and returned the farmstead to its rightful position as a show place. The Home Farm has become a designated centre for rare breeds of farm animals, preserving many varieties of cattle, pigs, sheep, goats and poultry which might otherwise be in danger of disappearing. Some of these now-rare animals would have been entirely commonplace on the Home Farm at the time it was built.

ELSEWHERE ON THE ESTATE

The other farms on the estate are working farms and are not open to the public, but many are visible from the roads and footpaths. Few are older than the seventeenth century, and all have considerably more recent additions to their fabric. Few cottages now belong to the estate, since most were sold off during the 1930s. The row of eighteenth- and early nineteenth-century cottages at Brick End, just above the Home Farm, is now in private hands. Of the various cottages which Soane designed in the 1790s, the only one which can now be definitely identified is the 'French House' on the east side of the main A14. (It is a private dwelling.) This was the cottage built of rammed earth or *pisé*, although the French of the cottage's name probably refers to the family who did most of the building works on the estate rather than the material. Many of the cottages at New Wimpole, built in the 1850s and '60s of bricks made on the estate, as well as the (now-closed) village school, are outstanding examples of the estate architectural style so common in the mid-Victorian years.

Many other buildings in Wimpole, Arrington and other nearby villages bear testimony to the influence and endowment of the Earls of Hardwicke: Kendall's Arrington gates, the Susan, Countess of Hardwicke Almshouses, the Hardwicke Arms inn, remodelled by Soane, the cottages at New Wimpole, the frequently rebuilt Arrington Bridge, and memorials and renovations in the village churches.

NOTES

1 M. Spufford, *Contrasting communities: English villagers in the sixteenth and seventeenth centuries* (1974), p.95; HMC, *Portland MSS*, vii (1901), p.385.

2 BL, Add MS 35679, fos 24 *et seq.*, Add MS35680, fo. 4, Add MS 35695, fo. 104v.

3 E. W. Brayley and J. Britton, *The beauties of England and Wales*, ii (1807), p.125.

4 Cam UL, Add MS 5819.

5 Herts RO, D/Ecd F106.

The Home Farm, built by Soane in the 1790s

BIBLIOGRAPHY

There are considerable manuscript and drawing collections relating to Wimpole Hall. A significant number of drawings and a few papers remain in the house. Many other drawings and papers are included in the collections of Sir John Soane's Museum. The principal manuscript collections are in the British Library, most notably the voluminous Hardwicke Papers, Additional MSS 35,349–36,278 and 45,030–45,047. Many of the Harley papers have been calendared by the Historical Manuscripts Commission or edited separately for their bibliophilic interest. Other family papers and estate papers and maps are housed in the Cambridgeshire, Hertfordshire, Bedfordshire and Cornwall Record Offices, Cambridge University Library, Victoria and Albert Museum, and the Library of the Society of Antiquaries.

The following books and articles have particular relevance to Wimpole and its history, or were especially useful in the preparation of this guide.

Country Life, 15 February 1908; 21, 28 May 1927; 30 November, 7, 14 December 1967; 6, 13 September 1979.

Royal Commission on Historical Monuments, *West Cambridgeshire* (1968).

C. R. Elrington (ed.), *Victoria County History: Cambridgeshire and the Isle of Ely*, v (1973), pp.263–72.

Historical Manuscripts Commission, *Bath MSS*, vols i (1904), iii (1908); *Portland MSS*, vols v–vii (1901); *Dartmouth MSS*, Report XV, Appendix i (1896).

Special issue of *Apollo*, September 1985: articles by John Harris, Arlene Meyer, and Brian Allen.

Special issue of *British Library Journal*, xv (1989): articles by Clyve Jones *et al.*, on Harley family papers.

BIDDULPH, Elizabeth P., *Charles Philip Yorke, 4th Earl of Hardwicke* (1910).

COLVIN, Howard M., *Biographical dictionary of British architects 1600–1840* (John Murray, 1978).

ELLISON, David (ed.), Alexander Campbell Yorke, *Wimpole as I knew it* (Bassingbourn, n.d. [1975]).

FRIEDMAN, Terry, *James Gibbs* (New Haven, 1984).

GODBER, Joyce, *The Marchioness Grey of Wrest Park*, Bedfordshire Historical Record Society, xlvii (1968).

GOOCH, William, *General view of the agriculture of Cambridgeshire* (1813)

HEYWORTH, Peter L. (ed.), *The letters of Humfrey Wanley: palaeographer, Anglo-Saxonist, librarian, 1672–1726* (Oxford, 1989).

JACKSON-STOPS, Gervase, *Wimpole Hall* (National Trust, 1979).

JACQUES, David, *Georgian gardens. The reign of nature* (1983).

PARRY, Eric, 'Wimpole Hall', *Architects' Journal*, 26 March 1986, pp.36–55.

PHIBBS, John L., *Wimpole Park, Cambridgeshire: a survey* (National Trust, 1980).

RUFFINIÈRE DU PREY, Pierre de la, *John Soane: the making of an architect* (Chicago, 1982).

RUFFINIÈRE DU PREY, Pierre de la, 'John Soane, Philip Yorke, and their quest for primitive architecture', *National Trust Studies 1979*, pp.28–38.

STROUD, Dorothy, *Sir John Soane, architect* (1984).

WILLIS, Peter, *Charles Bridgeman and the English landscape garden* (1977).

WALPOLE SOCIETY, vols xviii (1930), xx (1932), xxii (1934), xxiv (1936), xxvi (1938), xxix (1947) [George Vertue's notebooks].

WREN SOCIETY, vols xii (1935), xvii (1940).

YORKE, Philip C. (ed.), *Life and correspondence of Philip Yorke, Earl of Hardwicke*, 3 vols (1913).

INDEX